HEAR THE ART
visual poetry as sculpture

richard tipping

CONTENTS

Visual poetry as sculpture	5
A poet's start in the art life	7
Dearth	21
Alphabet Soup	30
Signs of Australia	34
Airpoet	36
Art Freeway	38
Poet Tree	40
Safe Art	43
The Eternal Question	47
Imaginaction	52
Shifting Ground, Cracked Wall	57
Road Works	59
Form 1 Planet	63
Smothered	67
Neoeon: New Age	70
Shouting Zone	72
Earth Heart, Hear the Art	76
Hearth	93
Division of the Sexes	99
Sounding Silence	102
The Relative	110
Sea Song	117
Watermark	123
Whispering Fence	133
Ooroo	139
Canberror	147
Writing on Electrons	153
Cosmic Seed	166
Acknowledgements	174

Copyright, 1977. Bluepearl granite, engraved, goldleaf. Diameter 7 x 2.7 cm. Edition of 7. One is in the collection of GOMA/QAG Brisbane.

VISUAL POETRY AS SCULPTURE

Putting together the words and images for this book has meant balancing emphasis and style between a survey of certain kinds of artworks and an illustrated memoir of some of my practice over decades. *Hear the Art* is both of these at the same time, and I hope that the reader will accept some unevenness in tone and detail in these stories of adventures in public art.

What this book is not includes small sculptures, assemblages, drawings, printed graphics and paintings.

Not art signs

There is little room here to discuss my extensive work in sign language including the *Roadsigned* series (1979 to the present), a genre for which I've become best known rather against my wishes. The *Roadsigned* works are represented by *Airpoet*, *Art Freeway*, *Form 1 Planet* and *Ooroo*; and other artsigns by *Danger: Postmodernism*, *Caution: Avant-garde*, and *Shouting Zone*.

Not engraved stones

Also excluded from discussion are the majority of *The Everlasting Stone* sculptures (1976 to the present) which embed single words or short phrases or typographic concrete poems in marble or granite, with the exception of *Moonday* and the large works *Dearth*, *The Eternal Question*, *Sounding Silence*, *Sea Song* and *Writing on Electrons*.

Not found signs

Very briefly discussed is the on-going photographic series *Signs of Australia* which document ambiguity and contradiction in the urban signscape. A collection of these was published by Penguin Books in 1982, and sold five thousand copies which was way ahead of possibilities for poetry book sales! Included here is only *Your Home Comes First* and *Beach Inspector*, giving context for *Airpoet*.

This book concentrates upon select pieces from a wide range of practice in a field which have I named word art work, and attempts to convey some of the complexity of relationships between visual and verbal aspects of a certain kind of typographic concrete poetry and textual objects where what was originally a page design becomes a physical entity in the context of a place. In attempting to elucidate and contextualise both materiality and variation in the development of my own body of work, I necessarily engage with the role of photography as both document and deed. Photography as a bridging medium has allowed the observations, constructions and interventions in public space to return to a reproducible and publishable form on paper equivalent to the printed poem.

One of the distinguishing aspects of my word art works is variations, or versions, whereby a conceptual design (sometimes a typographic concrete poem) is progressively made manifest in different forms through different materials and media over time, and changes in its nature and its audience. I don't consider any of this repetition, but the re-manifestation of core ideas in fresh form, and enjoy the differences.

Coming into art through poetry – that is, through an intense engagement with language itself – brings a 'literary looking' into the construction of 'artworks' and the social domain available for 'word art works'.

My interest has been to see if some of the innate qualities of poetry (density, potency, poignancy and memorability for example) could be 'translated' into objects which are accepted as art rather than literature. I say 'accepted' because these two worlds are just that: worlds apart. There is little cross-over in institutional support, critical reflection, and attractions of audience. This may because there are few examples of poets (that is, people with a track record in performing and publishing poetry in the 'poetry world') who are also artists using language as a fundamental ingredient of their art – and having that art exhibited and recognised in the 'art world'. Similarly, there are fences of definition set around photography which often exclude more than they include. It is not common for someone to be accepted across the borderlines of definition and technology as a multi-disciplinary practitioner. Reputation must be established afresh in each field, and what may be offered in the amalgam of new connections and dimensions can be dismissed as a lack of depth and commitment in any one domain.

There is a continuity of development in my practice which, while both multi-faceted and multi-media, follows its own paths from the printed page to public space, and back again. I have tried to foreground relevant processes of making work, and to show how the demands of different materials, scale and placement alter the work itself (originally an 'idea object', now something else). Each physical art-thing has its own way of being in the world and in the mind while sculpture demands its physical domain in the mortal arena.

Photography can bring us close to understanding what a sculptural work looks (or looked) like from a certain point of view, but cannot replace the bodily experience of dimensional space. This becomes more complex when in some cases photographic representation is all that remains of a work made to be public for only for a certain period so that afterwards it can only exist in the memory of participants and in its visual documentation.

I hope that some of the stories included may be of interest as primary material. Telling them makes me want to tell more since my work in the literary and visual arts, built over decades, has anything but a linear structure: it is a story full of loops and interwoven spirals illustrating how variations of a single work have made the one into many with qualitative differences; how photography has been an important ingredient in working between media; and how 'objectness' affects and effects textuality.

A POET'S START IN THE ART LIFE

My life in poetry took off in 1968. Responding to the Vietnam War and with the threat of being conscripted looming, I wrote political poems such as *Soft Riots / TV News* and read them at anti-war demonstrations in both Adelaide and Sydney on stages in front of thousands of people over the next few years. Poetry seemed to have a vital purpose. This poem is a riff on the war as a media event constantly fed into black and white television sets and published in colour.

Co-editing *Mok* poetry magazine with Rob Tillett in 1968-69, the print run of issue 5 was 1000 copies. An innovation by Rob was the extensive use of illustrations, including with the Soft Riots poem.

In 1969, when I was nineteen and had moved to Sydney for the year from my home city of Adelaide, I encountered Christo and Jean-Claude's *Wrapped Coast* at Little Bay. This event, made possible by John Kaldor, was constructed by a large team of volunteers including art students who my partner Betty Ross and I knew. We went to the site several times, and walked all over the headland and foreshore as the white fabric was being installed. It's hard to appreciate the scale from photographs: it was massively massive. Although this installation art had nothing to do with language I was inspired by its audacity and the way it drew attention to what was now not visible, making the ordinary extraordinary. This art said that it was possible to go beyond the confines and safety of the gallery, to think big, that it was okay to be temporary, and that the photography of art mattered.

> i tell ya jude
> you can't beat the sheriff

> che che che che
> che guevara
> che che guevara
> che che che guevara
> che che guevara
> che

> angelic hip christ holding
> bulletholes to his poems :
> crucified dead & buried
> after three days he didnt
> rise / no rock rolled back

Cover of *Mok Vol. 5*, 1969.

SOFT RIOTS

6pm july 4 1969

    theyre marching on the american consulate

        be/cause

    theres nowhere else to go

its cold in the city wind off the water
    trains on time

    marching
    marching for
    marching for reasons

in adelaide a man takes off his coat
in melbourne a man sits down and sighs
in sydney a man changes channels
in brisbane its windy southwest change max 65

    THE CAMERAMEN ARE READY action
                           action
    the spotlit streets   action
    spit back cats cars   action

a spearhead of radicals bearing red flags urged
on and led by other students a drawing of the prime
minister was also burned a petition police wielding
batons kicked and punched 1000 independence day
ball with 99 arrested and constable green hit by
a stone & allowed to leave

      i tell ye jude
      you cant beat the sheriff

        che che che che
         che guevara
        che che guevara
        che che che guevara
        che che guevara
        che

    angelic hip christ holding
    bulletholes to his poems :
    crucified dead & buried
    after three days he didnt
    rise / no rock rolled back

RICHARD TIPPING

TV NEWS

    who live out your lives
    who live out your lives
      in darkness
      in darkness

        a match
        three butts
        ashes all
        on a box
        of pins

the police were unable to find a motive for the killing.
they suggested three alternatives :

READY

    up against the wall
    they pin the target
    to your chest & share
    your last cigarette

    up against the wall
    clawing at

AIM

spotlights arclight gutteral swing bark
blinding the wire ripping through your outstretched
fingers tearing at your machinegun gut gut to
shredding clothes a shirt flagged above bones the
wire flashing with the sun wire barbs gas sssh ing

when i close my eyes its dark in my brain

zzzooooooooooooooooooooomm shot
    reversed to full screen
    panoramic wall

    strung by the hungry prisons of

FIRE

      click

    goodnight melbourne
    lights out adelaide
    brisbane shut your eyes
    sydney
      see you in the morning

Soft Riots / TV News, Mok magazine Vol. 5, 1969.

Christo, *Wrapped Coast* 1969 (detail). Photograph by John Clegg, from a print in the author's collection.

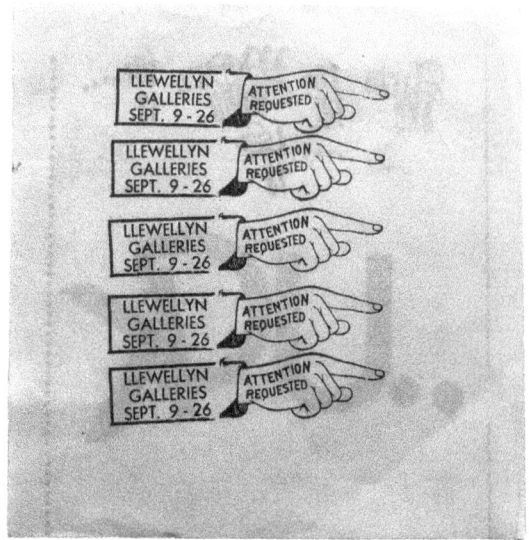 

Flyer for the Uck exhibition, 1970, designed by Aleks Danko.

In 1970, having moved back to Adelaide, I often hung out with students and staff at the South Australian School of Art where Betty was studying while I was busy with humanities (in drama, English and philosophy) at Flinders University.

One day I assisted Aleks Danko get ready to give an unofficial performance at Flinders. He was sprayed thickly all over his clothes with shaving cream and then wrapped in shiny aluminium foil which was poked full of little holes. As he walked slowly down the steps from the library to the main courtyard, worms of white goo poked their heads through his silver suit while he uttered declamatory provocations. Aleks invited me to share his first exhibition, at Llewellyn Galleries in Adelaide, saying that he did not have enough work to fill the space. I remember saying: "But I don't make art!" and his reply: "But you *could*". We decided to call the show Uck, in the spirit of *Mok* a poetry magazine which I'd been co-editing with Rob Tillett in Adelaide and then Sydney in 1968-69.

Aleks's sculptures included the *Log Dog* – a big wood log on little wheels with a collar and chain leash – and glass jars full of tampons with photo booth portraits of the artist. Many were bought for or have subsequently gone into public collections.

One of my works was a set of four large wooden cubes of the hardwood jarrah, whose twenty four facets each carried a word (made in Letraset, and sealed with varnish) starting with each letter of the alphabet, except X and Z. By rearranging the blocks, different sequences occurred. The viewer would handle and rearrange the blocks to make their own poem, including for example:

She is
a mutiplicate
of falters,

a butch
delicacy, offering
me wrigglecake or
cutting blackberries,

she is
enclosed against this

prickly Spring

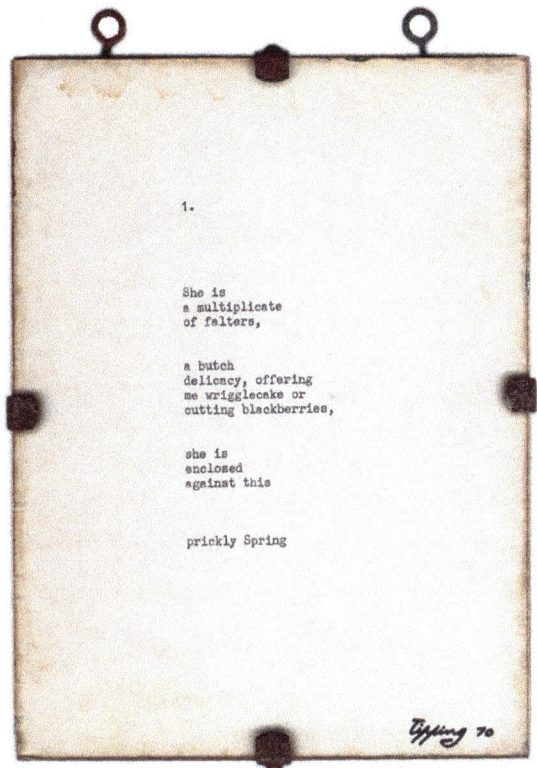

Framed poem from the *Multiple* series, 1970.

NAPALM	FOR	OUR	CHILDREN
MORE	QUIET	THAN	DEATH
LIKE	GENTLE	JUST	SADNESS
KILLED	IN	YOUR	UGLY
PEACE	BUT	WERE	RAINBOWS
EVEN	VIOLENT	AS	HOPE

With six faces each on four cubes which could be moved into different orders, the possible combinations of words in rearrangements were beyond my mathematical abilities to compute. This work was bought by Stephanie Britton, later to be publisher and editor of the important magazine *Artlink*. When I asked her about the block poem thirty years later she explained that it had ended up in her child's backyard sandpit and been lost. There is no photograph of it, simply the memory.

There was also a framed series of sixteen short poems from a sequence titled *Multiple* which I was writing at the time, intended as a portrait of a young woman, namely Betty. Each poem was meant to be interdependent in a multiplicity of reflections to make a complete picture. I framed hand-typed poems with no visual addition, just the bare typescript of the poem on the pure white of the page as 'canvas', each held in a homemade frame with clips holding glass to a thick backing board. My interest was in calling attention to the eye-movements of the reading process, to the 'reading' of pictures, with the line-breaks of the poems forcing the eye through certain tiny movements. Since the poems had no decorative elements it might encourage an appreciation of the poems as visual forms where the details of line break were a rhythmic device, replicating the hesitant patterns of natural speech. I was taking wall space in the gallery for poetry in its own right.

This attempt to bring poetry into the gallery and make words into art and art into words, both in and outside the gallery, one way or the other, ended up becoming a significant part of my life's work. The artwork in Australia resisted poetry for the same reasons that it was resisted by newspapers, television and even radio (except for a valiant programme here or there): it was seen as boring, or too difficult, or potentially embarrassing – at least that is how it seemed at the time. Poetry was never going to be popular: if you wanted popular, write songs.

The first poem in the series '*Multiple*' is typical in its attention to the minutiae of voicing with spoken thought tripping forward through a kind of edgy hesitance. The poem needs to be said aloud, voiced slowly, not just eye-scanned.

The poem sits in the frame, a part of this 'portrait' series, published the following year in *New Poetry* magazine in Sydney under the title *Dry Tap & Bucket*. To see the poem in the frame is completely different from finding it in a magazine. My copy of the *New Poetry* still feels fresh, while the framed poem has the patina of age – the paper's edges are browning, and there is rust on what were freshly chromed clips. This gives the poem as embodied in this way both a certain potency (as a conceptual intruder into an art space) and poignancy (held in a fading form as aging paper and frame). The typed poem is an integral part of an object which is historical, and has specific meanings in the development of a writer/artist's sensibility and practice, while the poem itself remains free to float away in the memory of the reader, or to be republished, relatively unencumbered by the fate of things in time. Significantly, the same issue of *New Poetry* (June 1971) contains an essay by Terry Sturm, *Perspective on Concrete Poetry*, which discusses typographic works by Eugen Gomringer, Dom Sylvester Houdard, Alan Riddell and Ian Hamilton Finlay. He begins with a broad definition:

'Meaning' in Concrete Poetry always seems to imply an aesthetic dimension. By focusing in a direct way on some primary aspects of language itself, Concrete Poetry challenges traditional assumptions about poetry, and raises important questions about the relationship between language and objects, about the nature of the medium which an artist chooses and its effect on a way a work of art communicates.

Given that I was already composing concrete poems on a manual typewriter, it surprises me now that I didn't at the time extend these visual verbal constructions from the page onto the wall into a form suitable for exhibition. For example, the poem *Seaside, Pregnant, Evening* (1968). In Adelaide the sun sets into the sea of St Vincent Gulf. Walking along a beach's edge at sunset I passed close to a woman in late pregnancy, standing with bare feet in the water, gazing out. Tears on her face were brushed with a golden light, carrying enduring mystery:

> tears are like waves
>
> and to have given all
>
> child weight of love

These thirteen words become three symmetrical 'tear' shapes using the Courier font on a manual typewriter (the letter arrangement needs a fixed font).

The plain spoken poem is not simply presented or re-presented or represented in its visual form, but qualitively changed by being iterated within a formal structure which is visually mimetic. This 'shape poem' belongs in a long international tradition brilliantly surveyed in Dick Higgin's book *Pattern Poetry*.

In a decision I have long regretted, at the last minute I dropped all of the visual concrete poems from my first book, *Soft Riots*.

My second exhibition was also shared with Aleks Danko at his invitation, at Watters Gallery in Sydney in 1973. (In the same year I was asked to tour with Russian poet Yevgeny Yevtushenko, reading his translations in Sydney Town Hall and at the Adelaide Festival Centre). Aleks and I named this show *Soft Riots*, using the title of my first book of poems which had recently been published by University of Queensland Press (in 1972).

```
     t
   ear
 sarel
ikewa
   ves


     a
   ndt
 ohave
 given
   all


     c
   hil
 dweig
 htofl
   ove
```

Seaside, Pregnant, Evening as a screenprint in the folio *Word Works*, 1979.

Poster for the exhibition *Soft Riots* at Watters Gallery, Sydney, in 1973, designed by Aleks Danko.

Soft Riots, University of Queensland Press, 1972.

Soft Riots, Painted, 1973. Photograph by John Delacour.

My exhibition was on the upper floor of the gallery, and Aleks on the ground. He installed a roll of clear wide plastic sheet which could be wound up and down with idea texts which we each wrote, communicating between floors.

I subjected copies of *Soft Riots* to variation. Copies were held between sheets of clear perspex, with castor wheels attached underneath (the *Coffee Table Edition*) or padlocked shut (the *Bibliophile's Edition*). There was a set of three copies of the book, painted crudely in different dripping colours leaving only some words showing. Another work had a copy of the poem *Mangoes* sealed in a glass jar with an audio cassette recording of a lusty reading of the poem, and a ripe mango which began slowly to rot. Another work was a large target with a copy of *Soft Riots* (held open by screws) which had been shot a few times with a rifle by gunsmith Hambly Clarke at the range at the back of his gunshop in central Adelaide. I'd asked him to shoot my image on the cove. When I went back to collect the book a few days later he said it was one of the hardest things he'd been asked to do. This from a man whose shop proudly showed photographs of himself with a variety of large dead feral pigs. Opening the book out made the bullets holes appear as if they are going both in and out of the text. In retrospect, it would have been better to simply place the shot book cover-up at the centre of the target, signalling the "death of the author" (of course we were reading Barthes).

The impetus in these works was questioning the book as a readable object, denying entry for the reader, or forcing a tangential relationship between text and object, almost as a test: would the art audience respond to works about bookness rather than read a book of poems? The answer seemed to be a resounding 'yes'. Most of the edition of twelve *Coffee Table Edition*'s sold, and so did the three examples of the *Bibliophile's Edition*'s, the painted books, the shot book Missed, and the jar with the poem *Mangoes*. With the painted books, the selective emphasis on parts of poems left between thick splashes of paint was a frontal attack

Soft Riots (Missed), 1973. Book shot three times through author's portrait, placed opened up on target, with painted text. Photograph by John Delacour.

Mangoes (with mango and sound recording), 1973. Photograph by John Delacour.

on the purity of the 'clean white page', and the book as a simple container. (Tom Phillip's extensive elaborations of select portions of text in *A Humument* first appeared in a trade edition in 1980, so I was not aware of his work at the time.)

Two of the works from the *Soft Riots* exhibition stand out as key steps in my approach to the visual and verbal in a sculptural mix.

The *Coffee Table Edition* of this book was made in a numbered but unsigned edition of twelve (the title was hand-written on a slip of paper glued onto the front cover) which were constructed with Aleks Danko's assistance. These sat together on a table in the gallery, looking ready for action either on or even as a coffee table. Thanks to the attached castor wheels, the book could be easily moved around to its 'best' position for viewing. The book had become a new kind of object: there was no longer any need to read it. The book can simply 'be there' as a curio, a conversation piece, an art trophy. As a book, *Soft Riots* was theoretically readable if you were willing to undo four little brass bolts holding the book between two perspex sheets, but to do this would imply an ownership' more intense than that attaching

Coffee Table Edition, 1973. 18.5 x 11.5 x 5 cm.

to the normal 'coffee table book', which lies in waiting, inviting its pages to be flipped. One friend did open up the sculpture in protest, insisting that it be read, but the resulting dissembled work was soon damaged and subsequently lost. Coffeetable books tend to have rich graphic qualities as their role is to offer immediate visual interest and gratification to the grazing reader, perhaps waiting while waiting for conversation to begin or resume. Additionally, they may function to show off the interests and tastes of the owner, as well the finer arts of photography, publishing and book design.

In general, books are small, cheap, light and portable. They are necessarily multiple. Poetry books typically do not have any graphic elements apart from the cover, and their typesetting. They also typically do not sell in large editions: five or six hundred copies sold is considered a real success. *Soft Riots* was no different. The *UQP Paperback Poets* series was an exciting initiative, bringing well presented books out at a low price. If five hundred or a thousand copies is seen as a small number in the larger world of book publishing, it is a huge number to consider for an editioned sculptural object. I can remember imagining printing an entire edition of a poetry book in this wheeled form – an absurdity, of course, a sardonic response to facing what seemed to be the impermeability of public apathy towards poetry. The decision to limit the *Coffee Table Edition* to twelve rested with the availability of copies of the book, and the costs and bother of manufacturing and assembling the additions of perspex, bolts and castor wheels. At the exhibition eight were sold, at $21 each, leaving me with one to keep and a few to give away. That was many years ago, and my copy is still in excellent working order.

How much is the *Coffee Table Edition* worth? I don't know, but certainly a lot more than the plain book. One recently sold through a Sydney gallery at a substantial price. After all, the *Coffee Table Edition* was originally priced as an artwork at 21 times the price of a copy of the book. The book became an art object, resting for its presence upon the potential of its content, rather than the experience of reading. It crossed into a new world, and became a floating point in the scale of collectable 'art' things.

What about the poems? Some have kept appearing in anthologies, more will resurface one day in a 'selected poems', but they did not need that particular publication (of *Soft Riots*, as a paperback) to arrive or survive. The *Coffee Table Edition*, on the other hand, is intensely and only itself. It is a sculpture about the culture of books, about 'bookness', rather than an artist's book: the book has been unbooked. Whereas the pleasure of an ordinary book is that it wants to be handled and read. And read again.

Also at the exhibition was the *Bibliophile's Edition*. This consisted of a copy of *Soft Riots* with a hole drilled through the cover on the middle right side, and a padlock though it clicked shut, all held in a perspex box with the title and "1/1 '73" engraved onto the lid. There were three made, although each was marked 1/1, to emphasise uniqueness and preciousness as qualities which the imagined bibliophile sought. Padlocking the books was inspired by hearing that the most desirable items for some bibliophiles are books which have never been read because their pages (in a 'French-fold' printing from long ago) have not been cut open along their outside edge, opening the folds. Here was a neat contradiction.

Bibliophile's Edition, 1973.
Photograph by John Delacour.

The bibliophile as the lover of books cannot open the pages to read the book without lowering its value, lessening its status as a 'virgin' text. It is like the conundrums of the *Bride with her Bachelors*. The keys to the three padlocks were thrown into Sydney Harbour near where I lived at that time in Birchgrove. I remember walking through the exhibition with one of the directors, Geoff Legge, and discussing what the prices should be. When it came to the *Bibliophile's Edition*, I said "$100", which was quite a lot of money then (you could rent a big terrace house in a Sydney suburb like Balmain for $60 a week). Geoff said that they wouldn't sell. I replied that the high price was an important part of the work, as it reflected the bibliophile's expectations. Only one copy of the *Bibliophile's Edition* was put on display, but all three of the edition sold on the first day. Perhaps the buyers were not told that there were three? Did this matter? The collector Clive Evatt QC was one of the bibliophiles, and when he nagged me years later – even if good humouredly – about this discrepancy, it lead me to thinking about the book as an object and therefore as a mortal thing. There's safety in having more copies. When he lent his Bibliophile's Edition for a mini-survey of my work called *Multiple Pleasures* at the Art Gallery of NSW in 1996, both the book and its box looked rather scuffed. I was glad to think that there were two other identical ones somewhere. Perhaps one was still in mint condition?

Who's the bibliophile now?

At Watters Gallery during the exhibition in 1973.
Photograph by John Delacour.

DEARTH

In 1976 I began working with scraps of marble and granite from a large stone yard in Adelaide, Monier Granite, exploring how ideas of poetry might be embodied in a monumental form. The manager, John Hall, was happy for me to take left-over scraps heaped in a corner of their large stone cutting yard. Over months, these were man-handled alone into the back of a ute and driven to the sanctity of my rented backyard in the inner suburbs.

Each piece had a polished face and hewn-sawn sides, and many had a roughened top like a crust of bread. They varied in size from something which could be put onto a mantelpiece, to heavy lengths only just liftable by a man alone. I didn't want to engrave selected lines of my poetry into the granite like a new kind of page, but to work with the existing forms of the marble and granite scraps and find words which might belong *in* them. Could a poem consist of only one word or a short phrase if it was made as rock-solid sculpture? What kinds of poem could these be in the context of their sudden monumentality, with the stone pieces no longer hefty tidbits of geological time but transformed into verbal markers, points of contemplation, idea catalysts. I wasn't making gravestones. The function and intention of the work should remain mysterious. Though I did make one work on an old marble gravestone: *Monday Night (Moonday)* where the base letters are the horizon of Adelaide's Mount Lofty Ranges above which a full moon is rising.

Monday Night (Moonday), 1977. Angaston marble with engraved text, 95 x 45.5 x 16.5 cm. Lettering by John Glasson. Collection of the Art Gallery of South Australia.

Polystyrene letters across the back wall of the Adelaide Festival Centre Gallery, 1978.

These ways of thinking about what word-artworks might be culminated in 1978 in my first solo exhibition *The Everlasting Stone* at the Adelaide Festival Centre Gallery.

The title came from Monier Granite's commercial product catalogue *The Everlasting Stone* published in 1976 which had been withdrawn and pulped as demanded by the State Government's Trades Practices Department on the grounds of misrepresentation since (and I quote): "Nothing lasts forever." The director of the Festival Centre, Silver Harris, suggested that large polystyrene letters with the title be put right across the large back wall of the gallery.

Included in this exhibition were for example *Copyright*, *Monday Night (Moonday)*, *Balls/Bulls* and my first large sculpture: *Dearth*.

At the Black Hill granite quarry in Sedan, SA, 1978.
Photograph by Robert McFarlane.

Belgian nuns viewing the granite edition of *Balls (Balls / Bulls)* Everlasting Stone exhibition, 1977.
Photograph by Robert McFarlane, 1978.

Dearth, 1977. Black granite with engraved text. Collection of the estate of Milton Moon.
Photograph by Robert McFarlane, 1978.

Helmut Schneider chiselling the letters of *Dearth*, Adelaide 1978.

I had received a grant from the South Australian Government to make a full-scale version of *Dearth* for the exhibition. The text was hand-cut into a large slab of black granite at Monier Granite by master mason Helmut Schneider.

After the exhibition *Dearth* sat in the front garden of my rented home in St Peters in Adelaide facing the street for most of 1978. After deciding to move to Sydney at the end of the following year I donated the sculpture to Flinders University with the support of Donald Brook who had initiated the Experimental Art Foundation (which made all the difference in my early life in art) and the director of the EAF, Noel Sheridan.

Noel Sheridan.

Dearth, 1978, parked in the front garden in 1979.

Nicholas Tipping with *Dearth* at Flinder's University in 1979.

On the back of the sculpture is a plaque which shows the sequence of words 'dear / earth / d-art / a-t / dea-th / ea-t / art / ear', making the sequences 'dear earth', 'art ear', 'dart at death' and more in a commingling of possibilities growing from that single word meaning the scarcity or lack of something, until the word flows into other possibilities as words within the word as a memorial to absence, to depths in the unspoken.

After more than forty years I wouldn't change a thing – except for the way in which *Dearth* is positioned and displayed at Flinders, which has bothered me ever since the University's construction crew cut me out of the picture. A day and time had been arranged for me to be on campus to supervise all aspects, but without notice they had installed it without consultation several hours before I arrived. The sculpture was buried more deeply than I had wanted (it has a metal frame as support on the its base which allows height) and lost some gravitas as a result. In those days the site was on lawn, which is now regenerated scrub. The goldleaf in the letters needs to be refreshed. Should the sculpture be re-sited? It's placed in a far away part of the campus, but perhaps this adds to the strangeness. An option is to engage with the University direct and work towards the creation of a 'sculpture walk' with paths and seats to make a contemplative space, a secluded nook. It would help if *Dearth* was mentioned anywhere on the University's website. Sculptures are like children: you're always looking out for their welfare even when they are older than you were when they were born.

Brass plaque on the back of the *Dearth* sculpture at Flinders University. 'This work of Imperial black granite quarried near Sedan, South Australia, was sponsored by the Government of South Australia and is the gift of the poet who was a student of the University.'

The view looking from the back of the sculpture towards ... a future path?

Dearth at Flinders University, 2022.

ALPHABET SOUP

In 1978 I was invited to submit a proposal to the first Performance Art Festival, *ACT 1*, in Canberra, 'an exhibition of performance and participatory art' directed by Ingo Kleinert in Canberra. I brought over from Adelaide a trailer loaded with the big white polystyrene letters which had been the title of *The Everlasting Stone* along the back wall of the Adelaide Festival Centre Gallery earlier that year. That show had been subtitled *Giving weight to words*, and consisted of heavy marble and granite scraps with short poetic texts. Casually, as an outsider to Canberra, it seemed appropriate that *The Everlasting Stone* would float in the nation's capital, turning Lake Burley Griffin into an alphabet soup. The team of *ACT 1* organised a fine boat. With the collaboration of spectators becoming participants, the letters were arranged and re-arranged in a sequence of evolving phrases before being loaded into a dinghy and rowed out a way, then released to form their own combinations. No-one seemed to worry about the fate of the letters later washing up along various shores of the lake and I have wondered what other words were formed as well as the letters' individual fates.

1. The opportunity, the environment offered, to release up-wind in the Lake, Canberra, on a public Sunday, 12 large white polystyrene letters, alphabet soup, as discovered in the baby's bowl, rearrangements of meaning by the breeze, particulars in the day's chance circumstances.

2. The letters arranged as THE EVERLASTING STONE (title of Monier Granite's rock catalogue) was the title of an exhibition of polished granite and marble pieces, each indelibly marked – carved or sand-blasted and coloured with leaf gold – monumental poetry in a word, maximum density of association, this whole speech before the mouth opens, to see the spoken, foreign as Arabic, recognise shape as sound and letters in sequence as a vehicle for the mind, through ear and eye, to fly off upon.

3. To start by laying out THE EVERLASTING STONE on the shore and to move through simple steps to SEA NOTHING TV STEEL, SEE NOTHING TV STEAL as minimal shift to demonstrate some possibilities, then move by dinghy to the point of release. That polystyrene floats seems the opposite physical character of granite, which will outlive the language.

Artist statement from the catalogue of *ACT 1*.

I'm grateful for permission to include six photographs taken by David Reid and donated to the National Gallery of Australia, Canberra, which tell the story.

The Everlasting Stone letters being rowed out into Lake Burley Griffin for *Alphabet Soup*, 1978.
Photograph by David Reid, courtesy of the National Gallery of Australia.

THE EVERLASTING STONE
THE EVERLASTINGTONE
THE EVERLASTING ONE
THE EVERLASTING ON
THE SEVER E LASTING T ON
THE SEVERE STING T ALON
THE EVEREST TALON SING
THESE RESTING LONE VAT
THE SEER STING LOVE TAN
THE SEES LOVER TIN TANG
THE SEA LOVER STING TEN
SEAT LOVER THING TENSE
SEA TV NOTHING STEEL (E)

SEA NOTHING TV STEEL
SEE NOTHING TV STEAL

The order of re-arrangement for the letters of *The Everlasting Stone*, as published in the catalogue for *ACT 1* in Canberra, 1978.

Lake Burley Griffin as *Alphabet Soup* in 1978.

Photographs above by David Reid, courtesy of the National Gallery of Australia.
Bottom left photograph by the author.

SIGNS OF AUSTRALIA

Since buying a single lens reflex camera (an Olympus OM1) in 1976 I had been photographing unusual or ironic language events in the landscape where words undermined or made ambiguous the visual image, involving some kind of gap between intention and effect, or oddities in the ordinary, or a subversive element undermining the apparently normal. In public space words kept coming into the picture through signs acting like characters with speaking parts. Seeking out relationships between a found text (any written element) and its context in the social world became central to my looking. I was restless for clues to other levels beyond obvious and literal appearance, for new ways of seeing the everyday.

Sometimes it was enough to simply document an irony: a large air conditioning unit has been placed through the head of the 'mother' in a highly stylised graphic accompanying the homily 'Your home comes first', painted on (what was in fact, although this is not obvious) the side of a large hardware shop.

Or a mysterious sign announcing the absence of the inspector of beaches as a lone gull flies by along the deserted beach at Bondi, early one morning.

After many thousands of kilometres of driving around the country looking for such rare instances I decided to make my own.

Bondi Beach, 1982.

Kent Town, Adelaide, 1978. *Signs of Australia*, Richard Tipping, Penguin Books, 1982.

AIRPOET

In 1979 I was living in the Adelaide suburb of Mile End near a main road which leads to the airport. The direction sign was distinctive: square-ish, bright blue, and with a big arrow pointing up. Late one night I drove to the sign, pulled my car up onto the footpath, climbed onto the bonnet and traced the 'R', then went home, made an 'E' in white vinyl tape of the right size on a blue reflective background, and drove back. It was two or three o'clock in the morning, very little traffic. I climbed up again and placed the 'E' over the 'R', so that it read 'AIRPOET'.

A month or so later I was standing on the footpath photographing the new sign, as was Mazie Karen Turner, and a man walking past asked (with some laconic redundancy): "Photographing it, are you?". He seemed to be a worker from a local factory, wearing overalls and a towelling hat and carrying a box of lunches from a nearby shop for his mates. I said: "Yes, know anything about it?" He answered: "It's a worker's Christmas present!", smiled and walked on. The Airpoet sign must have been popular with roadcrews, as I was told (having moved to Sydney again) that it remained unchanged for the best part of a year.

I realise now that this event was pivotal. The sign had become a part of the accepted vernacular of that place. It belonged there now as an idea. My lifelong commitment to an exploration of sign language in public signs was made right there.

Airpoet, Adelaide 1979, photographing the sign as a local worker walks by.

Airpoet on Burbridge Road (now Sir Donald Bradman Drive) at Mile End, Adelaide, 1979.

ART FREEWAY

In 1981 when I was included in the *First Australian Sculpture Triennial* in Melbourne my contribution included an unofficial extra. On a large 'start freeway' sign soon after an entrance to the South Eastern Freeway bringing traffic into the city centre, a square of green reflective tape was placed over the ST of START and a new free way was born. The close-up photo shows my faulty work in sticking on the reflective tape as I couldn't hang around long with the car pulled up in the emergency lane. You can't get this kind of tape off, and it must have been annoying for the road authorities to turn the 'art' back into 'start'. By phone the next day Alex Selenitsch told me that while driving to work at Melbourne University he'd passed a big Art Freeway sign which made the next couple of kilometres look completely different.

Art Freeway, Melbourne, 1981.

Art Freeway, Melbourne 1981. Green reflective tape added to an existing sign.

POET TREE

In 1979 I made (had made for me) a brass plaque as a prototype for an intended edition as well as a stencil-cut version for spray painting. Any tree marked with the plaque becomes a 'poet's tree', on one reading, or is itself the poet? The word poetry thus split might remind you of rustling pages and leafing through texts; the rising saps and juices of root, trunk, branch and crown; while the relentless grinding of paper mills crushes trees into mountains of paper mostly made to be read and thrown away. *Poet Tree* was meant as a call to action, to be inserted into the everyday and acted upon, with the National Trust morphing into the Natural Trust.

Poet Tree appears as part of a large screenprint *The Blood of the Poet* in my first folio of prints, *Airpoet: Word Works* (1979), stencilled onto a photograph of a magnificent eucalypt which is being chainsawed in an advertisement for 'STC, an Australian Company of ITT' from *The Bulletin* magazine which talks of "reforestation programmes using genetics to yield tomorrow's super trees". This appalling idea really got my blood up.

The Natural Trust, brass plaque, 1979. 8.2 x 10 cm.

The Blood of the Poet, 1979. Screenprint, 75 x 64 cm, edition of 20. This print is well described online in the collection of the British Museum, London, thanks to Stephen Coppel.

SAFE ART

Safe Art, 1980. Photographed at Powell Street Gallery, Melbourne, 1980. 35mm black and white film, scanned from negative and printed on archival paper, 2015 (edition of 2). 90 x 78.5 cm.

Safe Art was made in 1980. I wanted to make a safe as an artwork. ArtBank had just been formed, encouraging art bank robbers. After consulting the Yellow Pages and ringing around, I was invited to visit the CMI Safe Company about an hour's drive away from my home in North Bondi. Ken Berry and his three brothers proudly ran the company established by their father. CMI stands for Craftsmanship Means Immunity and the safes (as stated on the plaque) are guaranteed 'Thief Fire Explosive Resistant'. This sounded perfect. I explained that I needed a security safe with the words SAFE ART engraved into the metal, and that it was going to go to an exhibition in Melbourne called the Security Show at Melbourne University's art gallery, and that I was hoping they would make the safe and give it to me. After explaining that the safe would need to be specially constructed as the metal is drill-proof, the Berry brothers nonetheless agreed and the safe was completed on schedule.

Safe Art was transported at my cost to the Security Show, where it was rejected because the lift wasn't working. *The Australian* newspaper reported that it was "languishing somewhere in Victoria on the back of a truck".

Safe Art and *Unsafe Art*, 1980 and 2015, briefly together at the Redfern studio in 2015.

Tony Twigg reminded me that in 1980 he was working at the National Gallery in Canberra as the director James Mollison's personal assistant. James asked him to reply to a letter from me, politely refusing my request that the National Gallery send one or two of their newly-acquired gold treasures from Peru to lock inside the new safe.

Between 1980 and 1983 *Safe Art* was shown at Power Street Gallery (1980) and at the First Australian Sculpture Triennial (1981) in Melbourne; at the Art Gallery of South Australia (1982) in Adelaide; and at Roslyn Oxley9 Gallery (1983) in Sydney.

Safe Art was then stored with Grace Fine Art in Sydney until 1989 when it was accepted as a donation to the Art Gallery of New South Wales, with the gallery paying some outstanding storage costs. The safe was duly delivered, and I forgot about it for twenty years.

In 2012 while looking at the gallery's website I wondered why *Safe Art* wasn't listed in the collection along with other artworks pictured there. I emailed a senior curator about this and after some time received word that the gallery had mislaid the safe. Staff had looked everywhere, registration files had been checked, but there was no sign of it. Somehow *Safe Art* had disappeared. Either the artwork was literally lost in transit on its way to being accepted into this major public collection (though the transport company did find an exonerating delivery note) or was thrown out with the tea leaves once there. There was debate about whether to de-accession *Safe Art* as a work which may or may not have been held. Yes, de-accessioned. This may be the destiny of all safe art, and a potent conclusion for a conceptual artwork in a mystery unlikely ever to be solved.

Thirty five years later the same four brothers still ran the CMI Safe company. Ken Berry's first words when I rang were: "Hello Ric, it's been a while". Ken had kept an archive of CMI's safes and was able to provide examples of the 1980s company insignia and spin-dial so that the safe could be made again to the same design. The Art Gallery of New South Wales agreed to pay for the manufacture of one. I also took the chance to replicate *Safe Art*, making a pair. Their safe was engraved with the words UNSAFE ART and this is unlikely to be lost.

Unsafe Art, 1980/2015. Photograph by Chris Mansell at the Art Gallery of NSW, Sydney, 2019, in the exhibition *The Legacy of Marcel Duchamp*. Steel, enamel, aluminium, die-cast alloy satin finished, 20 cent coin. Base: 55 x 51.3 x 47.9 cm; Safe: 63.5 x 48.3 x 50.8 cm. Weight of safe: 153 kg.

Lowering the granite blocks into place on the banks of the River Torrens, 1982.

THE ETERNAL QUESTION

The Eternal Question was commissioned in 1981 for the 1982 *Adelaide Festival of Arts* by the director Jim Sharman. The granite was quarried at Black Hill, SA, and donated by Monier Granite with on-site installation for the Festival by Tillett Memorials. Traditional hand-cut lettering was made by stone mason John Glasson. The sculpture was placed near to the Festival Centre on the banks of the River Torrens.

Six large blocks of hewn black granite weighing a tonne each are placed in a circle of seven metres in diameter. Each has one word carved into its sides: *IS* or *IT* or *IF*. These three words stand for the essentials: *IT* for matter, *IS* for being, *IF* for mind. Approaching, walking around the circle of these blocks makes for an interweaving chant: "Is it if it is? It is if it is. Is it? Is if it? If if is it." and so on.

Letterpress print from *The Sydney Morning*, Vol. II, 1991.

There is a seventh central block laying flat which has carved into its surface a spiral which becomes a question mark. The block is compass-aligned, and in each corner is a carved symbol. The dot of the question mark faces west and represents the sun setting into St Vincents Gulf. The northern mark is an 'N' drawn as a broken spear. East is in the shape of a stylised emu track. South is the constellation known as the Southern Cross.

After the Festival, back at home in North Bondi, the Adelaide City Council wrote demanding that I remove the sculpture immediately from the banks of the River Torrens or it would be removed by Council at my cost. I replied offering the sculpture to the City for the nominal sum of $1000, a lot less than the cost of the granite alone. The Council refused and reiterated its demand.

Not knowing what to do with the sculpture now, I contacted the stone mason John Glasson who offered to make it a part of a small breakwater he was building with a friend near the town of Robe on the far south coast of South Australia to improve their fishing. This seemed like a positive solution, imagining visitors in the future wearing masks and snorkels to examine *The Eternal Question* piled up underwater all topsy-turvy. Just before the blocks were to be permanently moved to this watery location a letter arrived from the director of the Art Gallery of South Australia, Ron Radford. *The Eternal Question* had been selected for an upcoming exhibition titled *Recent Sculpture in South Australian*. The Gallery organised and paid for

The Eternal Question on the banks of the Torrens River at the Adelaide Festival of the Arts, 1982.

the removal of the sculpture from the banks of the River Torrens, placing it on land at the back of the Art Gallery where it stayed for many years. When the University of Adelaide next door to the gallery subsequently resumed this land, Ron Radford tried to convince Adelaide City Council to allow the sculpture to be installed on the wide strip along North Terrace in front of the Gallery but this was refused as there were other design plans. So the sculpture was moved to off-site storage.

In 2003 the Gallery loaned *The Eternal Question* to Adelaide City Council for installation in the central city location of Light Square, and a brass plaque was made acknowledging the donors and giving details on the sculpture.

In 2008 art-loving drinkers from a nearby pub began rocking some of the large blocks backwards and forwards until they several fell over onto the lawn. What great fun. A circular slate base was created with the blocks locked in.

The Eternal Question during the Adelaide Festival of the Arts, 1982.

Kai Tipping with *The Eternal Question* at the Art Gallery of South Australia, 1984.

The Eternal Question as a graphic, based upon a drawing which was used to engrave a granite maquette in 1981.

The Eternal Question in Light Square, Adelaide, since 2003.

IMAGINACTION

In 1980 Edmund Capon as director of the Art Gallery of New South Wales asked me to come up with a big concept for the front of the art gallery. Soon I presented a mock-up design for *IMAGINACTION*, with a single letter held in each of the twelve panels along the façade. I was imagining the new word 'imaginaction' as thinking in action, action images, the image as action, images becoming activated, ideas becoming actual. There was no response, and I forgot about it.

Eight years later (after a time which had included a couple of years in Europe and England and now having two young children and back in Sydney) in early 1988 I received a phone call out of the blue from the Art Gallery. "Hello, Richard? It's Jan. We'd like to go ahead with the opening bow." "Ah, what opening bow?" "For the front of the gallery, for the opening of the new wing". I'd never heard of any bow, but had the temerity to say: "Oh yes, *Imaginaction* with *Opening Bow* – you know, with the word IMAGINACTION right across the façade using cloth banners"

"Yes, well, I guess – can you just send a quote?"

Not only a quote, but thanks to the fabric knowledge of Caroline Jones whom I brought in as collaborator there was a small cloth sample sewn with the font design as well as a video with a built model showing how the huge bow, tied between the central pillars, would open when the bell cord was pulled. The plan was that, following this event, the bow would be removed and the one-word poem would remain. At our first meeting with the director and his staff everything was approved.

The cloth banners were sewn in a shadow font, with pale blue letters on red satin, with each banner 235 x 304 cm. Some of the

Mock up design for *IMAGINACTION* submitted to the Art Gallery of NSW in 1980.

gallery's 'picture frames' have grand bronze displays celebrating artists such as Giotto, Titian and Rembrandt while the majority are empty because times changed. Each of the frames was covered over by one letter. The word *imaginaction* was my invention – as far as I know, first use – but this is unlikely to be credited in the same way that many original artsign works are purloined without acknowledgement, eventually to become memes. Perhaps that is best thought of as some kind of compliment.

The giant bow was all primed to go, with a hanging bell-cord for the Premier to pull to open it, when a storm began to brew and a downpour loomed, bringing instructions for everything to be transferred inside from the marquees on the closed roadway forecourt. Catering for hundreds was rapidly moved, the storm broke, the bow became sodden wet, and the special opening bow effect couldn't happen.

A few days later we demonstrated how it would have been like for the director, some staff and a few puzzled passers-by and then removed the bow, leaving the twelve letters alone as planned. *IMAGINACTION* was realised as I'd originally intended, turning the entire gallery building into a one-word poem object. The director liked it so much that it remained in place for six months during 1988.

Caroline Jones and Richard Tipping, photograph by Mazie Turner, 1988.

Cloth design for letters of *IMAGINACTION* by Caroline Jones, 1988. 20.5 x 26.5 cm.

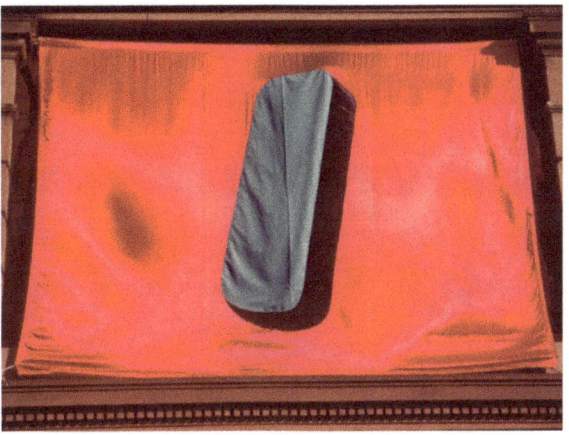

A cloth letter filling the sandstone frame.

IMAGINACTION from the Domain lawns, 1988. A family picnic perspective on the lawn.

IMAGINACTION along both sides of the façade of the Art Gallery of New South Wales, 1988.

The Art Gallery of New South Wales with *Imaginaction* installed, photographed from the Sydney Tower at a height of 300 metres. The Domain is crowded.

SHIFTING GROUND, CRACKED WALL

In 1989 I began a lectureship at the University in Newcastle. In December that year an earthquake badly affected the city and had a particularly negative impact on the art community through the loss of studio and exhibition spaces mostly located in the older parts of town. Suddenly Newcastle had become a disaster site with orange mesh blocking access to earthquake-damaged sites where walls of buildings leaned apart or showed their damage through lightning cracks on walls. *Shifting Ground* was a special foyer exhibition held in 1990 at the AGNSW to celebrate the Newcastle art community's resourcefulness in adapting and surviving. *Shifting Ground* was also the title of my front wall installation, intended as a spectacular shift to the appearance of the Gallery and bringing the earthquake into central Sydney. A large crack, from the roof of the right hand side of the gallery's front wall down to ground level, ran down between the names of Giotto and Raphael. This was accomplished by using a netting material onto which was sewn cloth in the shape of the crack in black, with an edge shadow effect. At the base, orange mesh sealed off the site, running parallel to the front wall. A reflective 'danger' sign SHIFTING GROUND gave its warning. The installation was accomplished in two weeks, from the idea and design to fabrication and rigging, and made possible by fax machines as well as the co-operation and goodwill of many people and organizations. Caroline Jones was the key collaborator again, a year after *IMAGINACTION*. The zig-zagging crack's design was based upon a crack in the wall of the Hidden Treasure Hotel, Newcastle, which was soon demolished.

Visitors to the Art Gallery of New South Wales this month may be shocked to see the impact of the Newcastle earthquake on the building. There's a huge jagged crack across the front but the Gallery is not about the collapse. Richard Tipping's Cracked Wall *on the front of the building makes a dramatic reference to the reality for many Newcastle artists. The earthquake which measured 5.5 on the Richter Scale severely damaged the central business district of Newcastle. It was here, in the oldest part of the city, that the majority of the Newcastle arts community was housed. Some thirty arts venues, from major galleries through to artists' studios and rehearsal space for performers, have been lost. In recognition of the sudden lack of resources the Hon. Peter Collins, Minister for the Arts, has initiated this exhibition to promote Newcastle artists and to assist in their re-establishment.*

Press release, AGNSW

Shifting Ground, 1990. Cloth installation on the façade of the Art Gallery of New South Wales.

ROAD WORKS

Road Works consisted of two double-sided banners made of vinyl fabric, each 18 metres long and one metre wide, installed on the Art Gallery Road Bridge over Cahill Expressway for the 9th Biennale of Sydney directed by Anthony Bond. The banners were on display from December 1992 to March 1993.

There is a line of text on each side making up a one-stanza poem in two couplets:

ART IS A PANE IN THE GLASS
TIME GOES BY IN GREAT BLASTS
NOW THE PAST IS AHEAD OF YOU
STONE COLD SOBER AT LAST

The plan was for rotation and replacement of the two banners across a four day cycle, so that each day a new line of the four-line poem appeared. However when the fourth line *STONE COLD SOBER AT LAST* was shown for the first time, that banner was stolen. Despite being picked up as a story through Column 8 in the *Sydney Morning Herald* the whereabouts of the banner was never discovered. I've imagined it decorating the fence in a long backyard, with a barbeque smoking and a cold keg being cracked. Thus for the rest of the Biennale, a single banner was rotated, allowing only half the poem.

Tipping is a concrete poet whose puns often embody significant ideas within their humour. In the Biennale he will be represented by a changing banner over the Cahill Expressway adjacent to the Gallery and bumper stickers that will be distributed by the Biennale and the artist.

Director's essay in the Biennale catalogue.

These Road Works *are for drivers and passengers going somewhere. I want their mouths to move, so that thoughts can be swallowed. They become the accidental audience, outside the framework of a gallery space or the national park of art (stuffed with endangered species, mining threats and environmental impacts.
We are as clockworked to our cities as bees to a hive. The view is at speed, through a moving window. If art is a pane in the glass, this is half of it. A hand on the wheel and a foot on the floor, swapping lanes, bumper to bumper. Each vehicle is a corpuscle, a self-contained reality bubble, flowing to or from the pumping urban heart, along arterial expressways, veins of roads, capillaries of streets and lanes and driveways. The audience is time-travelling with rear-vision mirrors showing flashes of disappearance and pursuit, mixing past and future. Time is so lumpy and inconsistent. Only memory can cut out the boring bits, just as history is a language net thrown backwards – relishing the appearances and interferences of words cutting into the view, adding comments and titles, maxims to chew, as we roar by, all but oblivious.*

Artist statement in the Biennale catalogue.

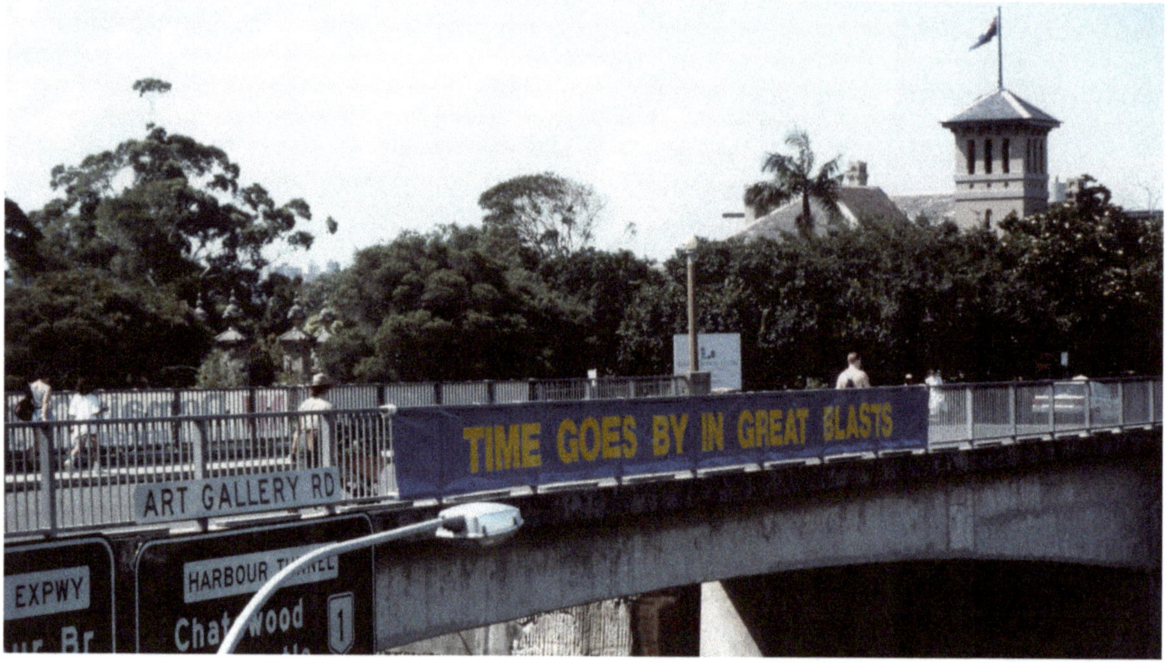
TIME GOES BY IN GREAT BLASTS
ART GALLERY RD
EXPWY
HARBOUR TUNNEL

NOW THE PAST IS AHEAD OF YOU
ALLERY RD
ARBOUR TUNNEL
atswood
ewcastle
1

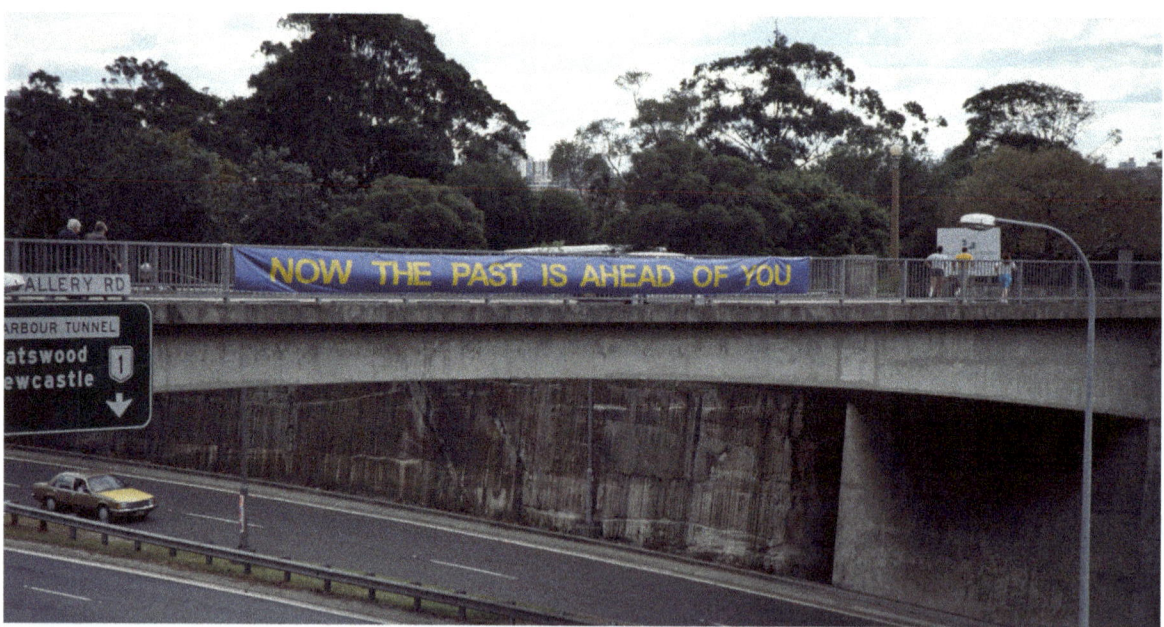

Opposite: Banners on the Art Gallery Road Bridge, for the Biennale of Sydney, 1992.

NO MORE CUNDING FUTS

Sticker for the Biennale of Sydney, 1992. 5 x 25 cm. Edition of 3000.

Art is a Pane, 1993. 19 x 19 x 8 cm. Glass brick with words engraved in reverse on the back.

Stone Cold Sober, 1996.

In 2017 Mark Themann as director of Latrobe Regional Gallery in Victoria visited my studio in Newcastle choosing works for a survey show and took a shine to the remaining banner, which had survived four or five house-moves intact except for a rat having chewed a few holes. We laid it out at its full 18 metres along the side of the building. He approved, and I had the banner repaired by a canvas specialist.

Now the Past is Ahead of You, 1992. One side of the remaining banner of *Road Works* stretched out at 18 metres length alongside the building where I was living in Newcastle at the time in 2017.

Now the Past is Ahead of You displayed at Latrobe Regional Art Gallery as a part of the survey exhibition Art Word, 2018.

FORM 1 PLANET

I had been planning to alter a Form 1 Lane sign since 1987 and had had one 'test' go at it on a sign near Darling Harbour in Sydney, which wasn't photographed. In May 1992 the P and T (purchased as professionally made stick-on vinyl letters for roadsigns) were added to a standard sign on Lake Road near Wangi Wangi at Lake Macquarie near to my family home. A photograph of this illegal linguistic intervention was included in the catalogue of the Biennale of Sydney that year when I was included in the core programme. The sign remained unchanged in situ for a long time because it was on a bend and easier to just let be and maybe the road crew kept 'forgetting' as they liked it. The image was also published in Art Monthly, *and on a T-shirt released by the Biennale. The idea has become ubiquitous. An edition of the manufactured sign, full size with pole, was announced and shown in the Biennale.* Form 1 Planet *was shown at the Chicago Art Fair by Tom Spender in 1993. One sold. Now what?*

From printed notes included with the folio of screenprints *The Sydney Morning*, Vol. 3, Thorny Devil Press, 1992, edition of 60.

The in situ photograph was included as one of a set of twenty four cards published as the catalogue for a survey exhibition at the Art Gallery of New South Wales in 1996 in an edition of 1000.

Manipulated sign, 1992.

Screenprint from *The Sydney Morning* folio, 1992.

Banner on the State Library of New South Wales, 2013-2014.

In 2013 the State Library of NSW made the screenprinted design as a banner to celebrate the exhibition *Born to Concrete*. This showing of visual concrete poetry was initiated by Heide Museum of Modern Art and then toured (with each adding works from their own collections) to Queensland University Art Gallery and the State Library of NSW. The banner was on display through the summer for three months, and is now in the collection of Newcastle Art Gallery.

In a recent twist, *Form 1 Planet* as a plain graphic representation of the altered road sign appeared briefly on the façade of Newcastle Art Gallery in 2021. This was on an advertising banner for the exhibition *The Art of Protest* in which the full-size aluminium *Form 1 Planet* sign from the Biennale of Sydney was included. The other artwork on the banner, *Coal is Over (If You Want It)* by Deborah Kelly – as a riff on John and Yoko's famous work – apparently raised the ire of a key player in the City Council's administrative staff who demanded its immediate removal. The message was seen as a political step too far in a coal-exporting city even for an exhibition titled, most ironically as a result of this censorship, the *Art of Protest*. The banner was removed as instructed, supposedly due to 'technical difficulties' and not replaced. A photograph by an artist passing by, who wishes to remain anonymous, allows the image to enter history.

Banner on the State Library of New South Wales, 2013-2014, shown from the reverse side.

Newcastle Art Gallery with *Form 1 Planet* in 2021 advertising *The Art of Protest*.

SMOTHERED

In 1992 I was talking by phone (from Wangi Wangi at Lake Macquarie, New South Wales, to Canberra) with the then Curator of Australian Art at the National Gallery of Australia, Mary Eagle. She mentioned an exhibition she was planning called *The Trial* and was looking for edgy, tense, disruptive takes on domestic life. I told her about an idea I had for a neon, which needed electronic timers to light its letters in different orders. This design had been conceived in 1980 and published that year in the literary magazine *Compass*, edited by Chris Mansell. I had recently made a graphic showing the animated changes as a screenprint in the folio of prints *The Sydney Morning, Vol. 1*, 1989.

I found myself saying to Mary Eagle the words within the word (without rearrangement, unlike an anagram) where 'smothered' becomes: smother / smothered / the / other / mother / mothered / here / there / her / red / moth. Mary asked me to send her one of the prints and a quote for making the neon.

This work was commissioned: a luxury. I worked with a local company in Newcastle, *Opalescent Signs*, deciding upon a long rectangle with a length of three metres and curved ends, and choosing a deep red glass for the neon. This was traditional English glass, which gives the best depth and tone (neon gas is a bright pale red colour when electrically charged).

The single word 'smothered' is shown to contain fragments of a scene (in a cinematic sense) containing worlds within a word. There are narrative traces, an imagined characterisation or interaction of 'characters'. There might be a "mother" who "smothered", whereas the "other" / "mother" / "mothered"; and either this was happening in two different places "here" and "there" or (reading further) the "here there" could be the flitting flight of "her" / "red" / "moth". Could the "red moth" be a "red mouth", thick with lipstick? The "red moth" could conjure an image redolent of crushed velvet, perhaps an enveloping cape, claustrophobic, or a suggestion of an escape? These are interpretative flights of fancy, no doubt. The word reveals its hidden interiors slowly, in a cyclic progression, with the red neon letters on their black background shining out across the open emptiness of a gallery floor.

The arrival of *Smothered* at the National Gallery of Australia was something of a drama. I thought (quite wrongly) that I was responsible for getting the artwork from Newcastle to Canberra, which meant a choice between a long drive each way or the significant cost of commercial art freight. In those days my family included three young children and I decided to save money by delivering the neon myself.

At the factory, *Smothered* was wrapped in protective bubblewrap and placed gently into the back of my old Holden Kingswood stationwagon, a big car but not big enough. *Smothered* had to be propped up on an angle, with perhaps 60 cm of the neon sticking out through the wind-down back window. After bringing it home to Wangi Wangi overnight, I drove to Canberra and stayed over at a friend's place, Stephen

Coppel, who was at that time Curator of Prints at the National Gallery and at his suggestion parked in his carport. The roof was not as long as the car with its cargo, and I should have backed in, as during the night heavy rain arrived. The next morning I drove to the National Gallery, and was cleared by their security to drive in to the loading dock. It was like finding yourself unexpectedly giving birth: lots of people suddenly appeared – curators, registrars, art-handlers with white gloves – and the work was carefully delivered into their hands from the womb of the old car. As it was being tilted up towards the waiting dock, water started to pour out: gushing water, a bucketful at least, splashing onto the concrete floor. Apparently a week went by before the neon sign was definitely dry enough inside for Gallery staff to be confident about turning it on.

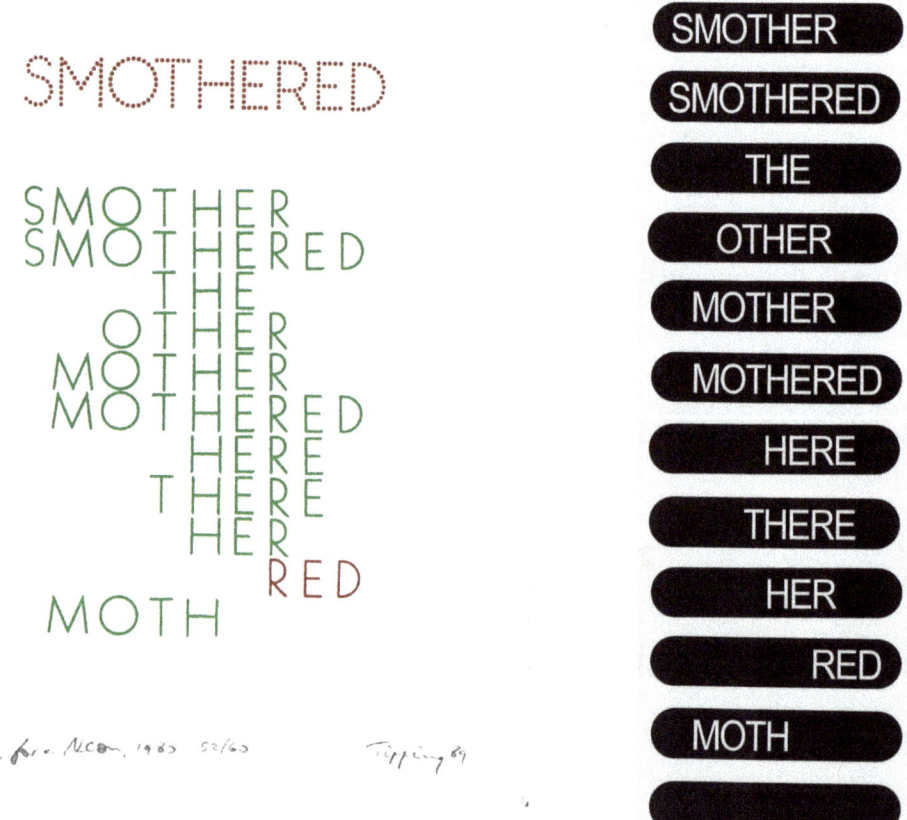

Screenprint from *The Sydney Morning Vol. 1*, 1989.

Smothered lighting sequence.

SMOTHERED

Smothered, 1992. Neon with changing text, width 3 metres.

The Kingswood parked near the studio at home in Wangi Wangi in 1991.

NEOEON: NEW AGE

Neoeon: New Age was commissioned by Monash University Museum of Art, Melbourne, for an exhibition of lightworks at MUMA in 1993, and made by *Opalescent* in Newcastle using pure yellow and pure blue glass tubing.

Neo (new) and Eon (aeon or eon, an indefinite and very long period of time) as NEOEON move slowly through changes in sequence in an animated neon. There is a glowering moody feel and a hand-made presence to neon which can't be imitated. In 1998 it appeared as a screenwork, an animated gif on my first website, but it was never intended as a screenwork per se. *Neoeon* is a light sculpture in the flesh, with its gravitas and slow changes three heartbeats apart.

This photograph is a screengrab from the MUMA website as I have no other image. MUMA could not afford the complete lighting sequence (each letter change requires an additional switch and these are expensive) so their version does not show the complete animation. The full changes are illustrated in this font by Emil Bertell which would be interesting to make as an LED lightwork (cutting out the shapes in sheet metal and placing programmed light emitting diodes in a metal box behind) as the colours and the sequencing can be varied to produce a series of iterations. Problem: now the 'neon' is not neon, how critical is that? Back to square one. Materiality and the malleability of meaning. Off the page and back again.

Neon tubing, steel, synthetic polymer paint, transformers, flasher unit, 120 x 120 x 18 cm.

Opposite: Lighting sequence for *Neoeon: New Age*.

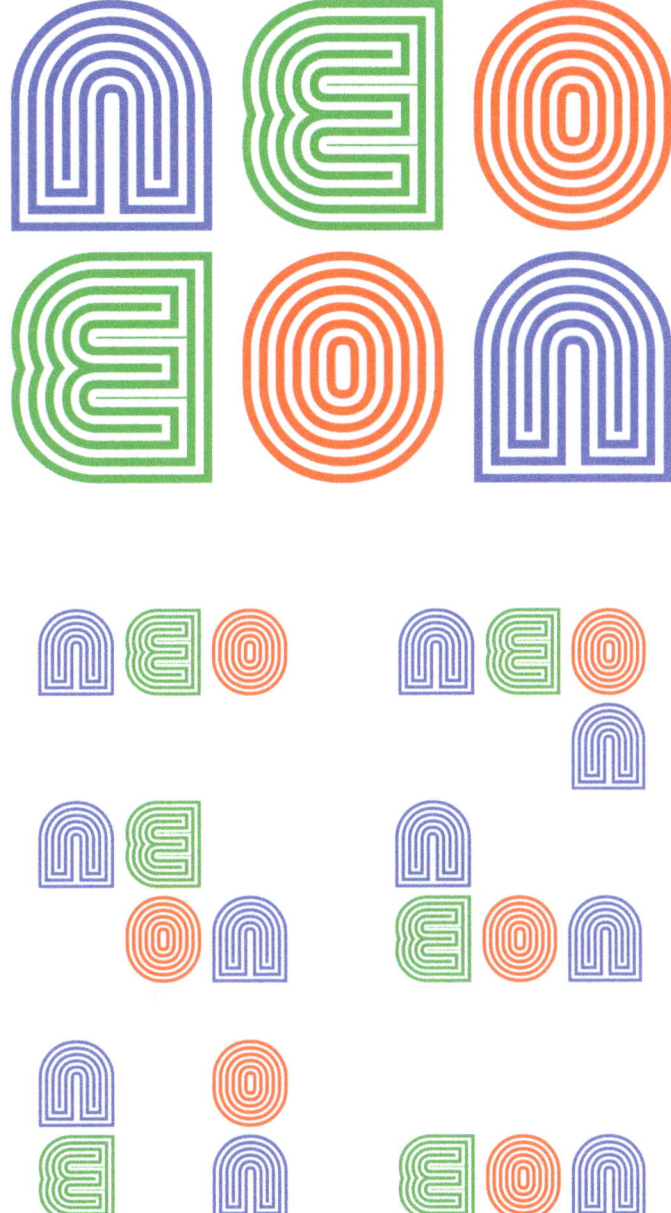

SHOUTING ZONE

In 1991 I was invited by Alex Selenitsch and Peter Herel to work in the Canberra Art School's Graphic Investigation Workshop. While mucking around with antique wooden types used for letterpress I came up with *Shouting Zone*.

A rapid ascent from patience to a parent's crescendo? The deafeningly rich silence of the desert? The rigid parade ground, empty of smiles?

This arrangement of wooden letters was printed letterpress by Les Petersen in an edition of sixty as one of twelve prints in the second volume of *The Sydney Morning print folios*.

A new manifestation of *Shouting Zone* appeared for the Australian Sculpture Triennial in Melbourne in 1993. The director David Hansen secured many interesting spaces across the city for a wide-ranging event lasting for weeks, and *Shouting Zone* was allocated a huge black wall in Melbourne's City Square on Swanston Street. The wall had once been a gigantic video screen in those analogue days. Unfortunately its use for entertainment and visual messaging had fallen foul of the City Council when someone broke in at the control centre, popped a pornographic video into the VHS machine, set it on repeat, pressed play, and chained the control centre shut.

The letters were hand-scaled from the letterpress design onto large sheets of corflute (the kind of corrugated plastic sheet often used for real estate signs) which is strong and lightweight. The letters were constructed from component parts, with the *T* being over 4 metres tall. On site they were attached in their sections to lengths of wood, lowered over the edge of the building and tied from inside with wire. Suddenly the street became a place where you could shout for silence.

The bold effect of *Shouting Zone* was enough to see it featured with an interview on SBS television in a short programme about the Triennial on *Dateline*. Usually such media effervescence vanishes into thin air, but the producer kindly sent both the original camera tape and a copy of the edited segment. These have recently been digitised, three decades later, and thus this temporary sculpture remains 'alive' for viewing, provided that the video finds somewhere to be seen. Websites are mortal too.

In the following year, 1994, working on another volume of the *Sydney Morning folio*, *Shouting Zone* was included as a screenprint.

In 2010, fifty were made in the USA in the opposite colour arrangement using vinyl tape on metal as an unsigned multiple and sold at zine fairs.

Letterpress print from the folio *The Sydney Morning, Vol. II*, 1991.

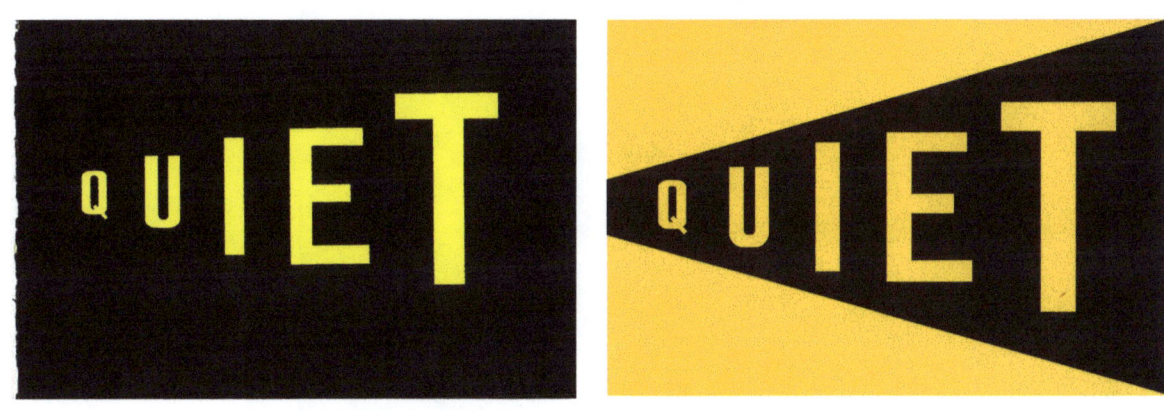

Screenprint from the folio *The Sydney Morning Vol IV*, 1994, 25 x 28 cm, edition of 60.

Metal edition, 2010, 175 x 25 mm.

Assembling the letters on the roof near to the display wall.

Shouting Zone in Swanston Street, Melbourne, 1991. As a footnote, the statue in the foreground is of explorers Robert O`Hara Burke and William John Wills, leaders of an ill-fated expedition of 1860 and 1861. This was the first statue cast in Australia.

Shouting Zone in Swanston Street, Melbourne, 1991.

EARTH HEART, HEAR THE ART

In the late 1970s I first saw the anthology *This Book is a Movie* (1971), and Alan Riddell's collection of concrete poems *Eclipse* (1972).

Earthearthearth (a title given here for convenience, it is not individually titled) by Ronald Johnson is from a set of poems called *The Songs of the Earth*. Johnson writes that: "Earthearthearth is a linkage of ear to hear and heart. Art and hearth are also hid in it." Johnson's block of repeated words is an aural mantra, resonant with layered echoes, shadows and depths – but what does the square signify? It is not a visual mandala (the word mandala is brilliantly treated in one of Riddell's concrete poems) but a sound poem. Alan Riddell's *Icon* is not one of his best concrete poems, as its shape – is it a square crucifix? – does not add to the effect of the words, and the addition of 'birth' seems unresolved. I drew my *Hear the Art* as a circle in 1993 with uneven letters and showed this to an academic colleague expert in fonts and page design software, Allan Morse, who quickly produced a version using the font Lithos. The circle is symmetrically satisfying and formalises the interpenetrations of HEART and EARTH four times each, with either H or E acting as a 'compass point' making an innate structure as the pattern of words and phrases emerge.

Using a black and white laser print-out of this letter circle as artwork, two colour screenprints were made. The variegation of colour within letters was produced physically by placing stripes of different inks before each 'pull' of the squeegee across the silk screen. Each print's colours vary as a consequence. The double-circle print was produced by cutting out the circles of letters from two black and white prints and pasting them together so that in only one instance of each circle is an 'R' on its side.

eartheartheath
eartheartheath
eartheartheath
eartheartheath
eartheartheath
eartheartheath

(Left) Ronald Johnson, from *Songs of the Earth*; (right) Alan Riddell, *Icon*, from *Eclipse*.

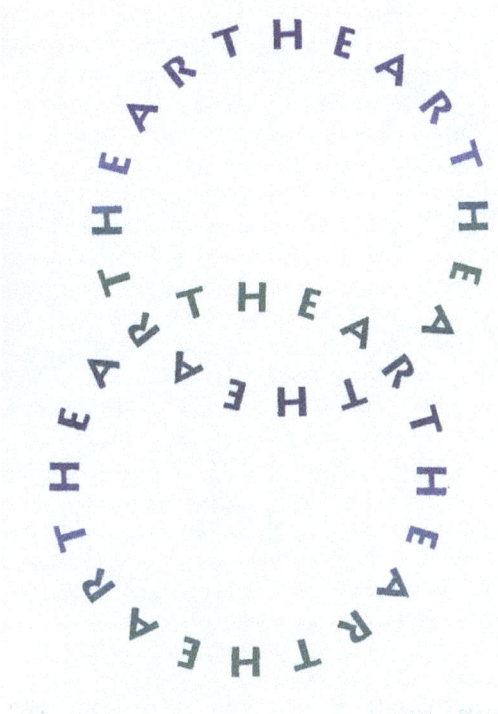

Hear the Art, 1994. Screenprint on cotton rag paper, 22 x 29 cm.

Hear the Art, (double circle) Screenprint, 1994.

These two versions with a single and a double circle were published in *Meanjin* magazine in 1996 along with a third version with five circles of the letters nested inside each other.

This literary representation was welcome, with the works as plain type able to sneak in as poetry because they had not become objects.

In the same year, I won a local sculpture competition with a proposal to make *Hear the Art* as a permanent installation in the gardens of Lake Macquarie City Art Gallery on the shores of a large saltwater lake over 30 kilometres long. (This gallery has been recently been renamed MAC Museum of Art and Culture). The plan was for a circle 24 metres in diameter with large trees in the centre to make a shaded bower over the next decades.

When the prize money was suddenly split between two winners the budget was half what I had expected and it was no longer possible to use small cubes of two kinds of granite with red for the edging and a speckled white for the centre. Instead, the letters were made of brick in two tones. There was no budget to pay a qualified bricklayer except for an on-site advice session so a lot was learned quickly the

Hear the Art, (five circles), 1994.

hard way working across an uneven sloping lawn with the crew being myself and family (especially my son Kai then aged sixteen) and a university student Joshua Thompson.

The design of the letters was extrapolated from A3 print-outs by traditional methods up to the full scale with a complex pattern of lines of string. The letter *R* presenting a special challenge in cutting these particular curves of edges on a screaming brick saw.

The resulting installation took weeks to make: marking out everything with string and then digging the twenty letters; placing several tonnes of pebbles and then packing sand in the trenches; trimming the edges of many bricks accurate to the typeface; and setting the twenty letters into a circle 24 metres in diameter.

Four photographs of the installation in 1996, (on page 80), show letters cut into the ground; filling letters with layers of base (pebbles, gravel, sand), and cutting bricks; working to set bricks into position.

To make the shaded grove of interwoven branches as a bower, six tuckeroos (cupaniopsis anarcardiodes) were planted in 1996 but these did not thrive because of salt spray sometimes blowing in from the nearby lake, I was told. The trees had received little attention and were replaced in the 2002 with four trees of another species. This change in the specifications of the sculpture from six trees to four was to accommodate the wide canopies of the new species, a kind of fig, but it may take fifty years before it will be clear whether this was a good decision.

In 2006 a simple flyer arrived in my letterbox at home in Newcastle from Aerial Impressions offering photographs of 'your house in your street'. I had long imagined seeing *Hear the Art* from the air, and thankfully the gallery then commissioned a photograph which shows the locale and scale of the work.

Although the sculpture is designed to walk around and within as a contemplative space and not as a something to be taken in with a glance, it could now be seen with a bird's eye view.

These days a view from the perspective of a satellite is available on Google Earth where everything everywhere in the world seems to be slowly becoming revealed. While surveillance coverage is not high resolution on the free version, you can even go '3D' and vary the angle of view. Just search for the gallery's location at Boolaroo, NSW.

After twenty five years in place the work is settling in for the long haul. This looping from a typographic concrete poem to a ground installation to the aerial view and back to the page is another marker in the drifts of materiality and scale of *Hear the Art* and its variations.

This poem was written for the park at Lake Macquarie.

Hear the Art (Earth Heart)

Earth's heart is sweet water –
blood, sap, rain and sea –
flowing in spirals of gravity.

Vast clouds sail past, reflecting
in a rippling blue lake of sky
their endless ideas for change.

You can feel each slow tree
by the green shore breathing
time's dappled shadows in.

Fresh weather. Swallows' wings
near pebble edges lapped by tide
quick dancing in the rising wind.

A photograph in the *Newcastle Herald*, with Jasper (10) and Grace (6), showing the original plan to use small granite blocks to make the twenty letters.

Joshua Thompson at work on *Hear the Art*.

Earth Heart (detail) at Lake Macquarie City Art Gallery, photographed in 2002 with new trees.

The grounds of MAC Museum of Art and Culture, photograph by *Aerial Impressions* 2006.

Photographs by
Gordon Elliott.

HEAR THE ART IN LONDON

In 1995 I was encouraged by the Australian High Commission's Cultural Officer, Rebecca Hossack, to make a proposal for a large-scale intervention on the exterior of Australia House in London to be installed as a part of a series of events entitled *newIMAGES: Australia and Britain into the Twenty First Century*. At first I imagined placing bright letters on transparent backgrounds into the many semicircular side windows of Australia House, which stretches as a triangular building along both the Strand and Aldwych streets.

Artwork proposal for Australia House, 1996.

Charles Levendosky, *Keystone*, photocopied lettering 1979.

In February 1997 the American avant-garde poet and critic Richard Koselanetz wrote to me after a meeting in New York, sending a photocopy of a work (left) called *Keystone* which, he said, Charles Levendosky had sent to him in 1979. "Once a prominent poet, he was recently a prize-winning editorial writer in Wyoming".

It's interesting that both my initial concept drawing (left) and Levendosky's design use similar fonts and were made as photocopies. Scanning equipment was relatively difficult to access in those days, and a lot of work was (and for me still is) accomplished with scissors, paper and glue. My own ideas for the Australia House meanwhile had developed past the semicircular to the circular, taking the entire front façade of this huge building as the 'canvas'.

The processes of solving technical problems, getting manufacturing quotes to fit budgets, clearing permissions with a mind-numbingly conservative set of government agencies within Westminster Council, and dealing with the Australian High Commission's own set of obstacles was in all a two year task involving patient bureaucratic mountaineering as an inevitable part in making public art. My own abilities in this field stem from years in the film industry where gumption, audacity, persistence and panache are assumed skills for producers and directors. Architects, bridge-builders and anyone else who wants to make big new things happen will know the feeling. Unlike buildings and bridges, however, public art such as *Hear the Art* on Australia House is temporary, with a strictly determined life. The permissions granted were for thirty days.

Laser-cut perspex letters edged with rope-light were attached to a grid of fine stainless-steel wire which was tensioned between the columns on the façade, thus avoiding any impact on the heritage-listed structure.

On the day of installation with the excellent Vanguard Engineering company, opening the crate of letters and wire on the footpath outside the High Commission we discovered that the manufacturer EM Signs in Newcastle had packed it in such a way that everything was now inextricably tangled, and instead of the specified grid of fine wire it had been made with only vertical wires. The boss of Vanguard drove us all to their factory a way away in London, a place so big that a full-sized fighter jet in one corner, rigged as if flying, looked like a toy. The riggers worked for hours to get the lightwork fixed, and we returned to Central London.

The installation crew were used to working as oil riggers in the North Sea, and climbed on narrow ladders without safety harnesses high above the street. We'd lost hours with the tangle and being November daylight was already fading at 3.30pm and it was starting to snow. The Deputy High Commissioner wanted to go home and asked if we could all come back tomorrow. I checked with the boss and passed on the news that they could return the next day for £3000. Permission was granted to continue, ah yes. We worked well into the deepening gloom of a November evening in thickening snow.

A microphone was fitted to the controllers of the rope-light, so that the brightness of the lights varied slightly according to the roar of traffic: a big red bus or a lorry swinging around the corner would cause a pulse, a fluttering of the heart (think of Duchamp's graphic *Coeurs Volants* which pulses with its red/blue clash).

This lightwork might have to gained more attention as an image if there had been publicity help but Rebecca Hossak's position as Cultural Officer's had just been abolished. *Hear the Art* received passing mentions in the London press but no photograph was published except in a news article in the *Canberra Times*. I was pleased with the shots I took with a 35mm camera, including the serendipity of the reflection of 'heart' in the balcony window. It would be 2002 before the image from London was otherwise seen in Australia, and that as a paid advertisement in *Art Monthly* for an exhibition at Greenaway Art Gallery which included a large photographic transparency of *Hear the Art* in a lightbox (150 x 120 cm). How else do these artworks exist, longer term, except through photography, that stealer of time and protector from fragility? Eventually this lightbox and another of the same size displaying these images became a part of the collection of MAC at Lake Macquarie. Also acquired were all of the letters and ropelight which arrived back as a charming tangle, deepening the representation of the London iteration.

Untangling letters at the Vanguard Engineering factory.

Installing on the High Commissioner's balcony at Australia House.

Hear the Art on Australia House, London, 1997.

Hear the Art on Australia House, London, 1997.

Two lightboxes showing *Hear the Art* in London, with the perspex letters and electric cabling. Collection of MAC Museum of Art and Culture. Photograph by Robert Cleworth.

HEAR THE ART AS NEON

In 1997 I was commissioned to make *Hear the Art* as a neon sign for a collector in New York. Timing switches (very expensive and heavy at the time) were hidden in the circular casing, and could be set to move at varying speeds within a sequence which runs through the permutations of earth / heart / hearth / hear / the / art. The neon is set in the rooftop garden of a penthouse on 5th Avenue, close to the Metropolitan Museum. In this photograph it is winter, daytime, and the neon is switched off.

Hear the Art, 1997. Neon with animated sequence, diameter 180 cm. Collection of Mel Meehan Oldenberg, New York.

HEAR THE ART IN GOLD

Prayer Wheel, 1998. Large wooden pattern from the BHP site in Newcastle, engraved text, fully covered in goldleaf. Diameter 104 cm. Swapped with Pat Corrigan for international freight costs, it is now in the collection of HOTA Home of the Arts, Gold Coast, Queensland. It was a crazy idea covering the entire surface with pure goldleaf. That's a lot of gold there.

HEAR THE ART IN SILVER

Earth Heart, 1998. Silver necklace made by Pierre Cavalan, diameter 16 cm, edition of three.

HEARTH

A drawing-together and culmination of many of these threads can be seen in *Hearth* (2007), which builds upon previous arrangements of the letters *H, E, A, R,* and *T* by making a formal word square. The geometric arrangement of letters does not have a pictorial or mimetic function but demonstrates innate formal structure, in an international tradition of word squares such as the famous *Enigma of Sator*.

The move from a circle or circles to a square is qualitative. The pleasure for me lies in the formal arrangement of the letters in diagonal stripes which reveal multiple readings bound in by the repetition of *Hearth* as the first and last letters of hearth with the corners locked. The repeatability in the structure, architectural in form, places balancing elements into a useful 'dwelling' upon core ideas which emerge from the six lines.

In 2007 *Hearth* was made as a series of wall works, each with 36 granite tiles engraved with a single letter and placed into a set of six stainless steel strips at a size of 180 cm square.

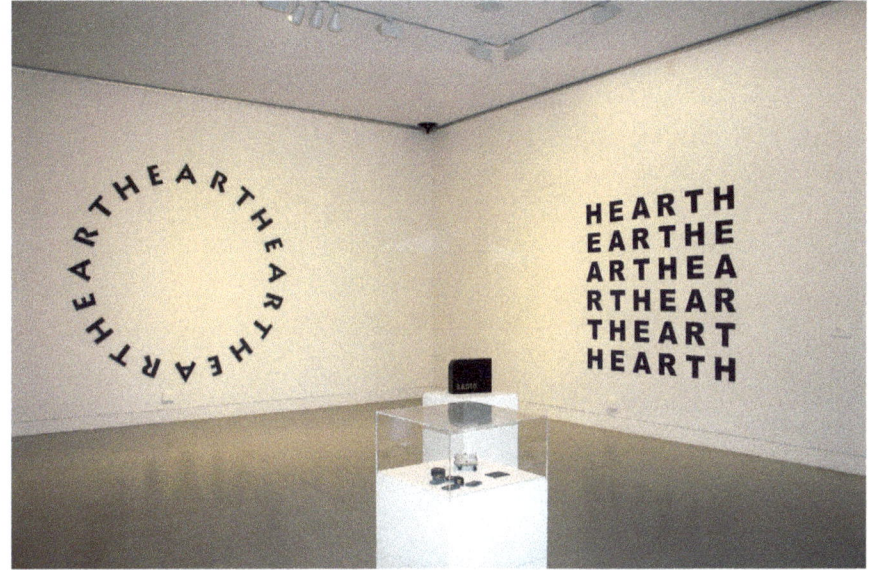 

Hear the Art (circle) and *Hearth* (square) at Lake Macquarie City Art Gallery, 2007, in the survey exhibition Multiple Choice.

Hearth, 2007, in three versions at Australian Galleries, Melbourne in 2008. Granite tiles, goldleaf, stainless steel rails, 180 x 180 x 3 cm.

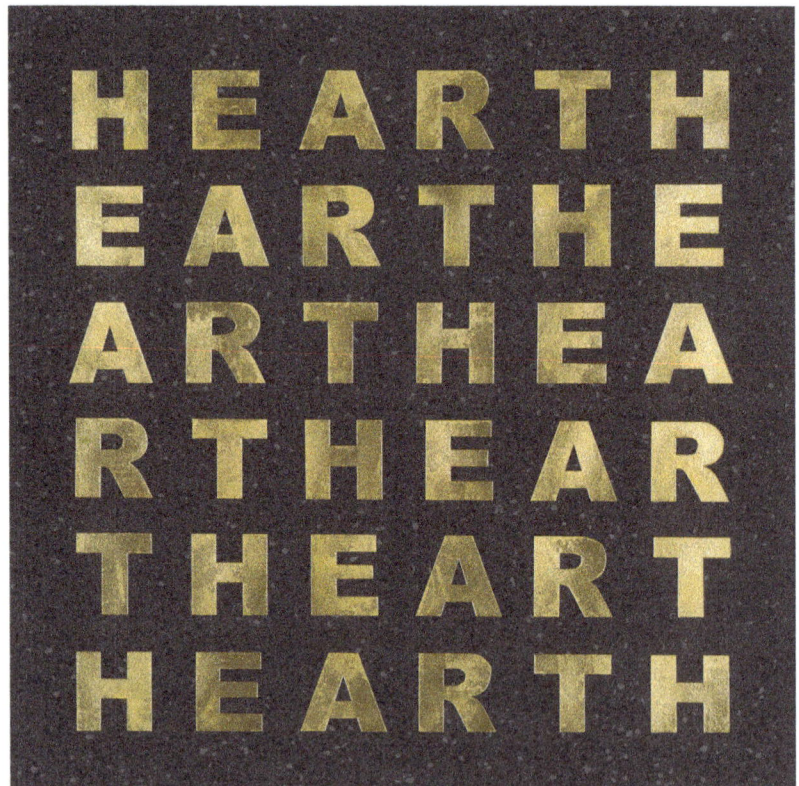

Hearth, 2008. Porcelain tile engraved and finished with goldleaf, 62.5 x 62.5 x 6.5 cm. Edition of three. Collection of ArtBank, 1/3.

HEARTH AT THE MITCHELL LIBRARY

Hearth installation at the State Library of NSW, 2013. Adhesive vinyl prints on the Dixon stairs to the Mitchell Library. Commissioned for the exhibition *Born to Concrete*, touring from Heide Museum of Modern Art, Melbourne.

HEARTH AS A LAWN WORK

For a temporary public artwork it's hard to beat using grass. In 2008 I was commissioned by Frankston City Council near Melbourne to come up with an idea for their *White Street* series of art projects, directed by artist Mark Themann. The solution was big, cheap and very green.

I installed a square word work in the lawns of the George Pentland Botanic Gardens 15 metres wide, using the cut-out letters of a stencil font. These letters were scaled up from A3 paper print-out to full scale measurements. The material was thick black builders' plastic sheet which has no light show-through so it would sun-starve the grass beneath.

The plan was that these segments would be secured to the lawn using weed mat pins (which are shaped like a letter U) and I calculated that over 900 of these pins were needed, weighing over 20 kilograms. I flew to Melbourne with the packs of pins and the cut plastic in suitcases. My son Jasper joined me at Flinders Street train station for the train ride to Frankston. On site with Mark we laid out the pattern using string, over 200 metres of it, in a grid fifteen metres square, and put in all of the weed mat pins. This took the three of us more than six hours, bending like emus while the Garden's birds watched on.

Melbourne had been in a long drought and strict water restrictions were in place, but the Gardens had its own bores so water was available. Over the next six weeks staff kept the grass between the letters on a fertiliser diet with constant watering. Then the pins and plastic were removed, and the grass was mown. Mark reported that waterbirds were delighted, walking all over the surface finding insects. He borrowed a cherry picker and brought it to the Gardens to get this high angle shot. Hearth lasted for months, slowly fading back into green as the grass grew again.

Laying out the string grid.

Hearth being mown at George Pentland Botanic Gardens, Frankston. Photographs by Mark Themann.

DIVISION OF THE SEXES

Division of the Sexes began its life drawn on paper and was then constructed on a computer screen in the mid 1990s. The letters are reversed in alternate columns, making a structure which can self-replicate if a mirror is held along its lines, perhaps comparable to an image of DNA modelling. There are sexes, there's sex, excess and exes mirroring each other.

In 1997, while preparing for an exhibition in London at Emma Hill's *Eagle Gallery*, I met with the sculptor Warren Langley who invited me to visit his factory *Ozone Glass*. The design I brought along was *Division of the Sexes*, and this was made in slump glass at a size of 200 cm tall. The photograph at the time shows me standing with it outside the factory. Soon it was boxed up and air-freighted to London for an exhibition at the *Eagle Gallery*, thanks to Pat Corrigan. What was I thinking? Way too optimistic. The result after the exhibition was a large sculpture with nowhere to go while my dealer looked for a sale; and no budget to send it home. A newly met Australian friend stepped in and offered to house it at his house in London, which was fine for a few years until a long struggle began to wrest it back and it finally returned to Australia in 2020.

Handling the brick creates animation with letters squeezing and pushing through each other in personal engagement.

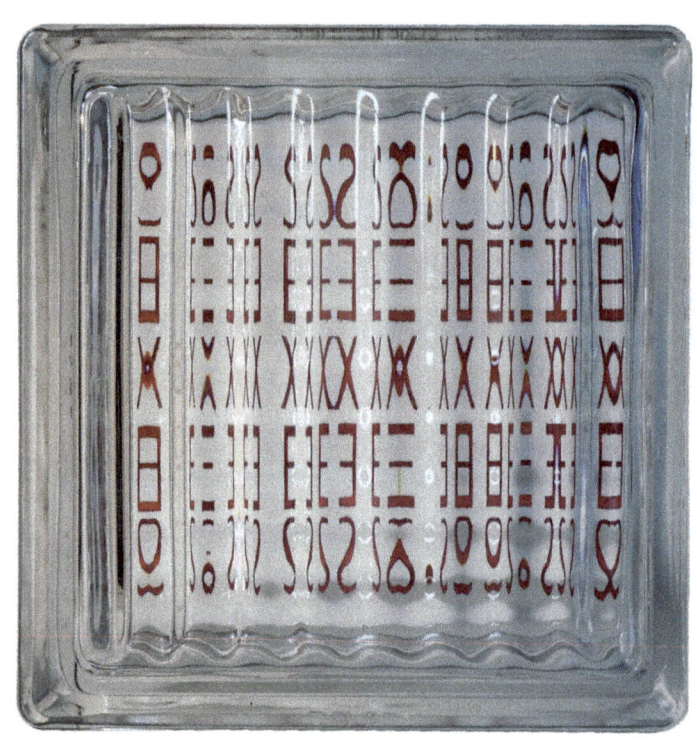

Division of the Sexes, 1998. 19 x 19 x 8 cm. Glass brick, engraved text with red paint on reverse.

Division of the Sexes outside *Ozone Glass* in 1997. Photograph by Warren Langley.

SOUNDING SILENCE

Poetry Is, 1994. Screenprint from the folio *The Sydney Morning Vol. IV*, 1994. Also made with black on reflective white vinyl on aluminium in various sizes since.

SOUNDING SILENCE IN TASMANIA

In 1995 I was invited to speak at a public art symposium called *Crossovers* in Launceston organised by the sculptor and curator Ray Norman, aimed in part at finding designs for artworks to commission for the city and including a tour of possible sites combined with practitioner talks by council staff. A highlight was the presence of two architects: Peter Edgeley who specialised in drawing up foggy concepts and capably demonstrating the impact of architectural visualising, and John Hall who was expert with ArchiCAD (computer-aided design) drawing. Both were at the artists' service.

Drawing by Peter Edgeley, 1995.

One of my proposals was for the sculpture which became *Watermark* in Brisbane three years later, (page 123). Another was a sculptural manifestation of a new anagram 'listen : silent' which would form the basis of the work I was eventually commissioned to make for Cataract Gorge in 1998. At first, I imagined the words set into a path, but where would this be?

Along the edge of one side of Launceston's famous Cataract Gorge is a late nineteenth century construct, a path held up by a criss-crossing wooden frames like the piers of a jetty, turning a rugged walk into a comfortable stroll, a promenade through wildness next to the South Esk River which sometimes roars loud and free, or patiently bubbles over stones. The Gorge was an Aboriginal haven. In the late nineteenth century dynamite was used to create a safe walkway through and it became a public park. This was an obvious place to begin.

The South Esk River near to the site of *Sounding Silence*.

As I walked up along the old path, a little boy ran ahead of his family and disappeared around the corner ahead. Soon he was back, calling out: "There's stairs, but there's nothing there!". A fine set of stone steps lead to a now empty rock platform with the toilets gone: a perfect place for sculpture: how could I resist? The resulting proposal was chosen and work began.

A cube of local Ben Lomond granite was hand-cut into a boulder shape and sliced in two like the halves of a metal-casting mould. Then the two words and *X //* were inscribed in positive and negative view and finished with goldleaf held tight on a paint undercoat. The work done by the Dunn Stone company in getting the sculpture up those narrow stone steps was exemplary and it still surprises me that it was possible. The sculpture was funded by the Australia Council's Public Art Fund, the University of Tasmania and Launceston City Council. Now, after decades in the weather, the goldleafing needs to be refreshed.

LISTEN and *SILENT* as an anagram each have the same letters, each word within the other. Many anagrams are mundane, even if amusing, while this one sings as if the words want to be together, morphing inside each other.

In this visual poem the words are connected by an *X* and a *//* showing the movement of letters in the transposition and transformation of meaning. The *X* and *//* make the Latin numeral *XII* for twelve, which is the total number of letters. The *X* and *//* also represent, respectively, both closure and openness, negative and positive, no and yes, stop and go, like binary code of *X* and *O* in computing, and the alternation of attention and expression in a conversation, with pauses between. Is silence really golden? John Cage pointed out that there is no such thing as silence for us: in the depths of a sound-suppressed environment you start to hear your own heart beat and your nervous system hum.

With the lettering on one half of the granite boulder reversed, the pair are like the two halves of a huge metal-casting mould, from which the original solid gold letters have dropped.

>The river is always talking.
>
>Listening. Stilling the mind.
>
>Breathing. Being right here.

In the following photographs the granite looks blue like the gorgeous Blue Pearl granite from Finland used in *Copyright* (page 4), but scanning a small sample – trade-named 'Tequila', as supplied by the stone company – shows granular felspar and quartz with rich pink and grey tones. This detail reminds me of the gap between the thing itself and images of the thing. Some of sculpture's grip on us is precisely that it is here, now, in our way, seen and felt, in its place with us, literally an experience in inhabited space.

Sounding Silence, 1998. Half way up the stairs to the rock platform.

Two sides of the sculpture.

Scan of a sample of the granite used for *Sounding Silence*.

Zephrin, Jasper and Rhapsody – one son and two grandsons on site in 2020. Photo by Jzhonnie Bechet Lumiere. Jasper was with me during the construction of the sculpture in 1998, aged twelve. The wide angle lens of a phone camera has produced some distortion in the apparent shape of the granite, which is more oval like the wall sculpture on the following page.

Listen Silent, 1998/2000. 41 x 32 x 3 cm. Engraved text on granite, goldleaf. Around six were made.

SOUNDING SILENCE AS A LIGHTWORK

Commissioned by Clive Evatt QC (1931 to 2018), *Sounding Silence* was on display in his personal art collection across four floors of the Supreme Court of New South Wales in Macquarie Street in Sydney for many years in the early 2000s. Unexpectedly, the sculpture came up for sale in a clearance auction of Aboriginal art from Clive's Hogarth Gallery in Sydney where it was out of context and was rescued at a bargain price. The fluorescent bulbs and internal fan were replaced with LED lights in 2020, and it was then donated to the collection of Newcastle Art Gallery by Richard Perram and Stephen Cassidy.

Sounding Silence, 1996. Raised perspex letters on metal sheet in a metal box with fluorescent bulbs. On display in the Supreme Court, Sydney, 2010.

THE RELATIVE

Albert Einstein's famous equation $E=MC^2$ is now commonly repeated, to the point of cliche, although few of us who can say "energy equals mass multiplied by the speed of light squared" have more than the vaguest idea what this all means. We do know that Einstein's Theory of Relativity, and this equation, lead in some way – accelerated by the Second World War – to the splitting of the atom whose most obvious consequence was the use in warfare of atomic bombs. The concept of the 'speed of light' alone is daunting, with its suggestion of vast spaces between stars and galaxies in an expanding universe and the consequent shrinking of our own scale, as 'thinking animals' marooned on a tiny sphere of rock with a molten core, surrounded by dark matter and dark energy.

$E=MC^2$ became an iconic marker of the twentieth century, like something which you can hold and rub, even while understanding that the equation which you are repeating could bring the entire planet to nothingness. In this sculpture the equation has arrived as a human-like figure, an idol which may be both a totemic ancestor and a space traveller, held between figurative form and linguistic object. *The Relative* could symbolise all of our relatives, both our ancestors and our descendants yet to be born, millennia into the future; a culmination of all the small steps which brought the human species to expressing relativity as a phenomenon of space and time.

The initial design for *The Relative* was made in 1984 when Mazie Turner and I and our son Kai were living at a studio at Besozzo, north of Milan, courtesy of the Australia Council. We had no materials to hand. I dreamed up the arrangement and drew it, turning the letters for the equation into a human-like figure, then found a supply of stick-on lettering in a local newsagent with a bold typeface and added dimensional lines.

At first the design had the M on its side to give vertical strength. The zigzag effect of the sideways M appealed for its unusual shape but I wasn't satisfied and the project went no further. A note written in 1986 while living in Oxford says: "By placing the letters in an unexpected relationship, a human figure akin to tribal sculpture is formed, standing unaware of the mathematical formulation which is 'genetically' contained in the body. The figure is monolithic, totemic, with the obsessive quality of a Sepic sculpture."

Design of the original drawing made in Italy in 1984.

In 1991 I cut out a 30 cm high model of this design in plywood using a scroll-saw, in what would become a common method of making word-things over the next ten years. In 1994 an Arts Design Industry Award from the NSW Ministry for the Arts allowed work with a metal fabrication company near my home at Lake Macquarie (an opportunity offered in association with sculptor Roger McFarlane) to make examples from steel sheet. At the factory a programmed plasma-cutter produced a small-scale model around 40 cm tall as a single piece which was then welded onto a circular metal base, and then a large version. This was purchased by the University of Newcastle where I was working as a lecturer in media arts, and this first design version of *The Relative* may still be standing near the science lecture theatre as an anonymous anomaly.

I had realised that placing a solid second sheet behind the first gave vertical strength as a spine so that the figure could be free-standing. Like many simple solutions this had taken a long time to discover.

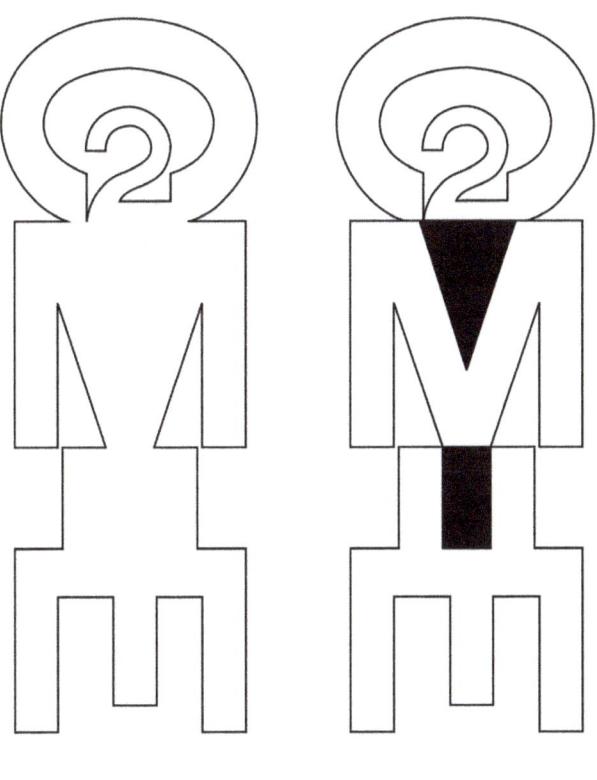

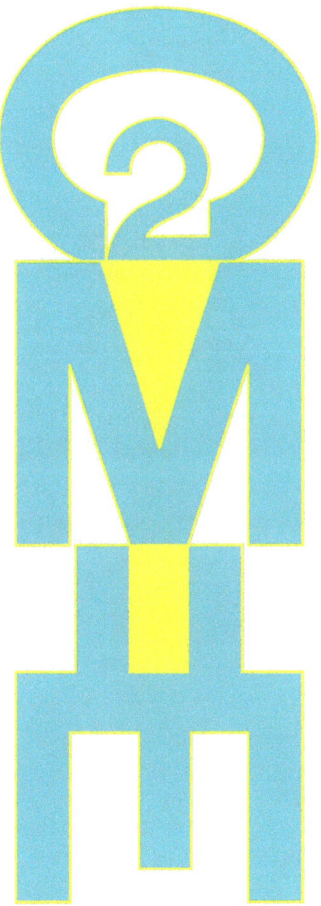

Computer drawings showing the solid sheet (left side), and then with three separate letters added on top.

111

In 1998, preparing for an exhibition at Ubu Gallery in New York, I returned to the steel fabrication company to make *The Relative* in three parts in stainless steel. This time *The Relative* was a typical adult size of 173 cm tall. Two large sets were made, and two small. Stainless steel had always seemed sunny, bright and hard as a new knife blade, but I learned that it needed to be carefully prepared unlike having something chromed. There are various grades and kinds of stainless steel: it seems tough and everlasting, but can also be a delicate substance with inscrutable characteristics. The steel has varying depths of sheen and tone according to how it is brushed and polished with fine-grained pads. I had learned techniques of hand-polishing stainless steel from Max who ran a small metal fabrication factory at Lake Macquarie. It took hours of brushing with ultra-fine papers, and handling with gloves once it was polished, to give a warm silver glow.

I cut three timber variations with a electric scroll saw from the lid of an old piano. These varnished veneered timbers have the presence of 'piano-ness', of played music hidden in their grain. Other timbers were also used for different maquettes.

In 1999 I was invited by David Sequeira to install commissioned works in the two lifts (elevators) of the National Gallery of Australia in Canberra. I named it *Art Lifts: Lifting Art*, and the Gallery used this title for subsequent commissions by other artists as *Art Lifts*. The plan was to make the lifts an odd pair in mood and appearance with the atmosphere in each memorably different. The left one would be cheerful in colour, filled with bright stickers as a background for two reflective signs; while the right one would be matt black and sombre with *The Relative* in polished stainless steel screwed onto the side walls and the back wall. The fluorescent lights in the dark lift would give the letters an eerie presence.

In the left lift hundreds of small octagonal 'Stop Go' stickers covered the walls and ceiling as a background for two signs facing each other: *Danger: Postmodernism doesn't give a flying duck* and *Caution: there is no avant-garde only those who have been left behind*. Passengers in this lift were to be overwhelmed with the 'messages' from which there was no escape but to look at the door of the lift which had remained plain stainless steel. In publicity there was reference to "a trickster whose quirky manipulations undermine language, meaning and authority", and in the gallery's *Art On View* magazine; "wry slogans in the form of construction signs humorously deflate the self-importance of art criticism".

The other lift was especially painted black. The stainless steel *Relatives* freshly returned from New York, two large and one small, stared from the walls. As the door closed, their presence became luminous, ominous, reflecting the lift's cold fluorescent light.

Photographs in this case can do no more than document the broad design of the installation: they cannot duplicate the experience of walking into one of the lifts and having the door close automatically, forcing people into a close engagement. One set of these stainless steel sets used for wall-mounting, as well as large prints of the installation photographs, are now in the collection of Maitland Regional Art Gallery, New South Wales.

The Relative, 1998. Scroll-cut from the wood of an old piano, 47 x 29 x 18 cm.

National Gallery director Brian Kennedy with Richard Tipping in the 'signs' lift in 1999. Scanned from the NGA's *Art on View* magazine.

The Relative (large and small) in one lift at the National Gallery of Australia, 1999.

In 2003, I proposed a version of *The Relative* as a free-standing figure for *Sculpture by the Sea's* annual exhibition at Bondi in Sydney, using the one of the two sets of large stainless steel letters. A kitchen manufacturer cut the various parts to make a plywood structure eight-layers thick to a depth of 20 cm. The three stainless steel letters were then screwed on, and extra wood was added beneath the legs of the E to raise its height nearer to my own height of 188 cm. After a lot of hand sanding and many layers of shellac it glowed with a dark rich patina.

In the studio working on *The Relative* in 2003.

Packing *The Relative* ready for transport to Sculpture by the Sea in 2003.

SEA SONG

The fascination with the words which can be found within words included a sculpture made in 1979, *S tone S*. I brought this volcanic beach stone back to Adelaide from a visit to New Zealand in 1977 where I had found it near the town of Napier. When exhibited at Robin Gibson Gallery in Sydney in 1980 it was shown on a circular mirror (as a part of the finished work) and purchased as such by the Art Gallery of New South Wales, where it was exhibited in my survey exhibition *Multiple Pleasures* in 1996.

This photograph shows its feel and heft. My interest in discussing *S tone S* is twofold: firstly, its origins lie like *Heartheart*'s in my discovery of the long poem *The Songs of the Earth* by the American poet Ronald Johnson. Johnson's poem includes the 'eartheartheart' as a square of letters previously discussed. The following page of Johnson's poem is this:

```
s  tone  s
s  tone  s
s  tone  s
s  tone  s

C  L  O  U  D
A  L  O  U  D
A  L  O  U  D
A  L  O  U  D
A  L  O  U  D
A  L  O  U  D
```

dark behind and
dark beyond and

underneathunder

Ronald Johnson, from *The Songs of the Earth*, in This Book is a Movie: An Exhibition of Language Art & Visual Poetry, Dell, New York, 1971.

S tone S, 1979. Engraved beach stone. 5.5 x 20.5 x 8 cm. Collection of the Art Gallery of New South Wales, Sydney.

This is a blueprint for the way the poem should be spoken, not a visual poem per se. The opening up of the word 'stones' to reveal 'tone' (where tone is understood as a way of sounding, modulation or intonation of the voice which is expressive of some meaning or feeling or vibration) is followed by a block of 'cloud' and 'aloud'. This does not have visual elegance but functions to create a cascading 'loud/aloud/cloud' which seems to be bringing in thunder with the glowering dark. In a statement preceding the poem, Johnson gives his own tone to the work:

"These songs are listenings, as poems must listen and sing simultaneously. Even the stones here have overtones and the clouds may speak."

My response to this inspiration was renewed in late 1998, when I wrote a sequence of words which would open in the same ways and reveal something akin to a sense of landscape in time and season. The six words

clouds / stones / grains / glistening / beached / pebbles

become as each word opens to reveal its inner sound

c loud s / s tone s / g rain s / g listen ing / b each ed / p ebb les

loud / tone / rain / listen / each / ebb

Significantly, this is a seascape, not a contemplation arising from absorbed and contemplated silences in the depths of the woods like Thoreau, as quoted by Johnson, but from walking in the wildness of some Australian beaches where it is easy to find oneself completely alone. The sequence is not static but has the dynamic interactions of the sea's littoral zone. My feelings from this set of twelve words within six are ones of hugeness, the scale of the sea piled up with burgeoning clouds, and the long beach stretching away into mist. You are walking, noticing the glisten on beach pebbles, perhaps you pick one up and feel its wet weight in your hand, and then hurl it back into the sea to be washed up again on the next tide. The swoosh of the spent waves sucking back on 'each ebb', and a sense of tides. The sound of rain, filled emptiness.

In 2001 I took the idea further, moving in scale from hand-sized stones collected from a beach in South Australia to small boulders, wanting to make an installation sculpture big enough to occupy serious space on a gallery floor. This bringing of natural found objects from far-away places into the safety and seeming sanctity of an art gallery has been the *raison d'etre* of Richard Long since the 1970s. Long takes photographs of paths and arrangements of stones made on his hikes to wilderness places, and then brings some of these back to urban domains where they sit in galleries. If this is a British version of *Land Art*, it includes Hamish Fulton and Andy Goldsworthy. Each of these artists works in their distinctive way with photographs and descriptive titles drawn from their notebooks. None of them would want to use words placed physically within their landscapes: this would be anathema, I would guess,

Sea Song, 1998. Six beach pebbles, shown at Ubu Gallery, New York.

a kind of despoiling of the contemplation. Their attachment to language is as a reflective entity adding authenticity to their responses to the landscape. Words appear in Long's and Fulton's books next to photographs, or (certainly for Fulton) as texts made of vinyl lettering on gallery walls. I mention these three artists because of their sensibility for the vitality of place.

The beach where I was able to get the small boulders I sought is near Nelson Bay, north of Newcastle, and is made only of stones, unusually for Australia. Big storms over the years have thrown them like commas and full stops into a littoral plethora of punctuation marks.

On the beach there are only worn, rounded shapes, the sea's playthings. I was very selective in taking some because stones have certain locales and meanings within what Hamish Fulton calls their 'homeland'. The stones (or boulders, or rocks, as you wish) belong there. A sea eagle was circling above the headland. There was no one else all afternoon.

Sea Song is a meditation growing from memories of long empty beaches aching into mist, of huge wind-shaped sandhills, and a surging endless sea. This was my early boyhood, on summer holidays near Encounter Bay in South Australia. I would sometimes accompany my father salmon fishing at daybreak, at a beach called Waitpinga, which had only one wobbly road in at one end. You could watch the whole length of the beach, miles of it, disappearing into a mist of seaspray from the booming surf.

I decided to include small beach stones as a circular base two metres in diameter, and to place the six engraved stones in their own circle onto that. Each engraved stone is approximately 30 cm long, by 15 to 20 cm wide.

I bought old ammunition boxes and was able to make the sculpture 'storable' in these four wooden chests. This is not an incidental detail, but an essential part of the concept of the sculpture as a transportable 'environmental marker'. There is an intense presence generated by the stones both big and small which cannot be conveyed easily in a photograph. This is an installation artwork, creating its own space in display, and then able to be packed away, to reassembled in a future occasion as a kind of unique publication, a repeatable archive of engraved landscape.

For the photographs, I sprayed the stones with water (recommending, without success, to Lake Macquarie City Art Gallery where they were shown in 2001 that they should be sprayed occasionally by an attendant with a fine spray bottle) and tried to capture the changes as the sun dried them off. The sculpture is now in the collection of Heide Museum of Modern Art, Melbourne.

Sea Song is a call to the silences which are in the centre of sound, to the stillness at the heart of movement, to the mysteries of voicing written language. It is also a kind of song in itself, as the sounds of the twelve words flow through each other, reminding us of this phonetic alphabet's innate music.

I imagined taking a trailer-load of stones from the beach, engraving them with the six words of *Sea Song*, and bringing them all back, placing them in their nooks and crannies to rejoin their fellow stones in the overthrows and reach of tides and waves, anonymous and ancient, and mysteriously inscribed.

Sea Song 2001, in its four old ammunition boxes used for storage.

A beach near Nelson Bay, NSW, the source of stones used for *Sea Song*, 2001.

g rain s, 2001. One of six engraved stones.

c loud s   s tone s   g rain s   g listen ing   b each ed   p ebb les
loud   tone   rain   listen   each   ebb

Sea Song 2001, six large engraved stones on a bed of beach pebbles, diameter 200 cm, at Australian Galleries Sydney in 2008. Now in the collection of Heide Museum of Modern Art, Melbourne.

WATERMARK

Giving weight to words, and seeing letters as sculptural forms, mirrors the ways we make thought concrete. Our words become shapes which reflect the energies we speak, and the ideas and passions which they contain.

From a statement for *Watermark*, 2000.

The design for *Watermark* developed during a public art forum to which I was invited in Launceston in 1995, as discussed in the section on *Sounding Silence*, (page 102).

The architect Peter Edgeley's drawing is rough and ready, but shows the effectiveness of his quick-drawn visualisation, and, perspicaciously, the scale which would eventuate in Brisbane when this seed became a large steel sculpture five years later.

The process of CAD drawing was exhilarating to me at the time in 1995, as simple as it may look now. The letters could be turned in dimensional space as if objects, and the perspective of shadows followed settings of the sun's position, and then overlaid on a photograph giving an impression of location, scale and perspective.

When asked to submit ideas in a competition for public artworks for the Brisbane Powerhouse Centre for the Live Arts in 1999, I was in New York with a solo exhibition at Ubu Gallery. I had made an on-line catalogue for the Ubu exhibition but then found that very few people in New York were accessing the internet in 1998 (things were very different in Berlin).

Watermark on 2 January 2011, detail of a snap from *Sundae Brisbane's Photos* on Facebook. Two weeks later the sculpture became the high water mark for major floods.

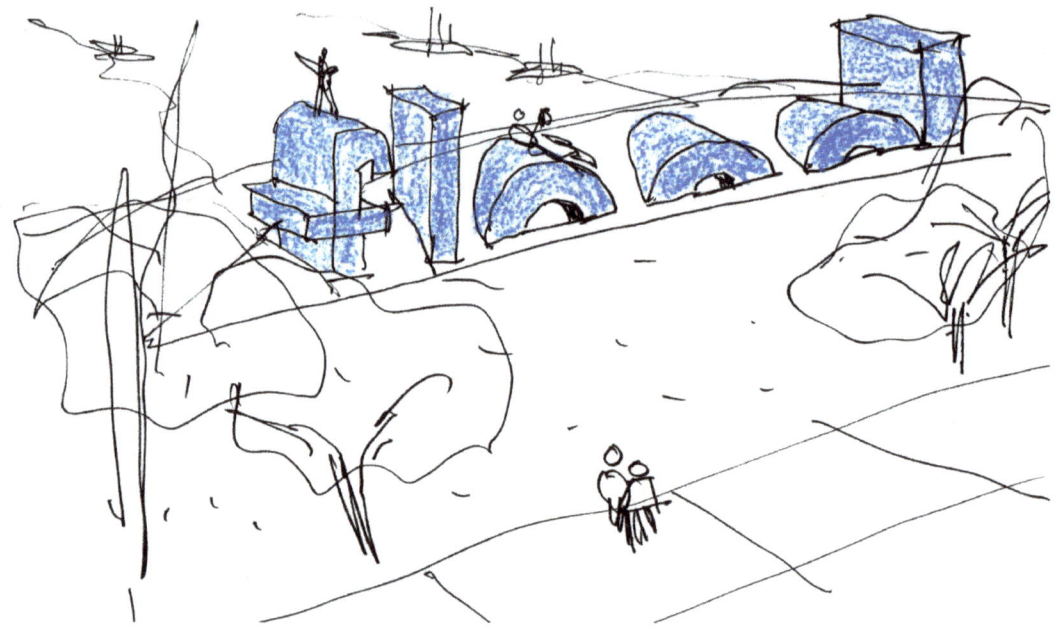

One of several 'Flood' drawings (architectural visualisations) by Peter Edgeley, Launceston, 1995.

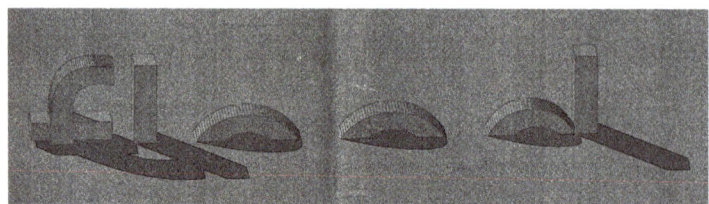

'Flood', two CAD (computer-aided design) drawings by John Hall, Launceston, 1995.

Watermark ('Flood') line drawing in Helvetica lowercase italic, 1999.

Maquette for *Watermark*. Wood.

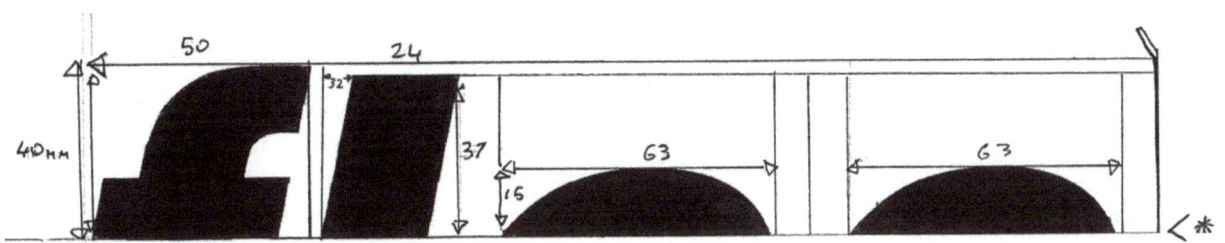

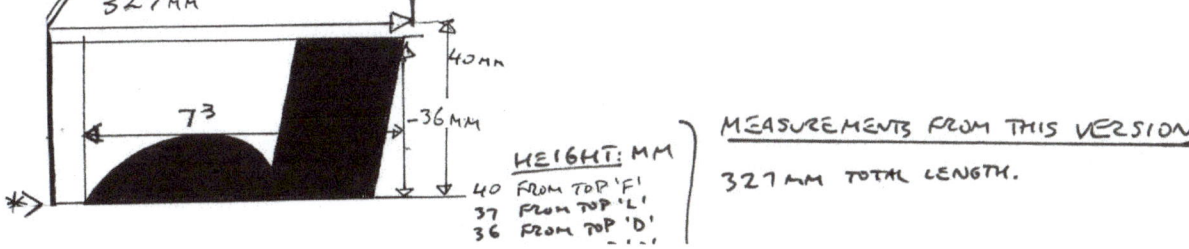

Watermark ('Flood') drawing, calculating proportional scale of the individual letters with a print-out and a fine ruler.

This sojourn meant that I was removed from my studio and did not have easy access to files, tools, and facilities, or to my files. I had never seen the abandoned power station at New Farm on the Brisbane River, but knew the area through visits to Brisbane over the years. I decided to enter Stage 1 of the possible commission with a brainstorm, generating pages of ideas, and using the materials to hand: a borrowed computer and printer, scissors and paste, and a fax (facsimile) machine. Although email was possible, the fax machine still ruled for general use and had the advantage of reliability unlike files attached to emails at that time. I printed out and then photocopy-enlarged the word "flood", cut this to shape with scissors and stuck it onto one of the master sheets as a fax.

On my return to Australia I was invited to visit the site to further develop a proposal (Stage 2). The day's meeting started well, with twelve selected artists joined by architects, engineers, council representatives and the curators. The huge old building had become a 'shooting gallery' for drugs and a place for 'rave parties' in recent years, and contained memorable and colourful graffiti murals. It seemed that these and at least traces of the gigantic machinery should be retained: so how was our work to relate to it all? After a tour of the building wearing safety hats, where the artists shared their enthusiasms and ideas freely, there was a formal meeting at which it became clear that only four artists would be commissioned. That shouldn't have been a surprise, but the atmosphere chilled somewhat and cross-fertilisation ceased.

Following my submission of further designs, the concept for *Watermark* was accepted and I was one of the artists chosen to develop their work to full design and budget (Stage 3) in order to – hopefully – move to commission (Stage 4). In my allocated role I was officially designated as the *Sensory Interventionist*, and developed other projects including one for an installation of new signworks to be installed in the precinct of the Powerhouse, which eventuated in 2001. (I won't show any of these here, as my many artsigns will be the subject of another book.) Meanwhile, I learned about steel manufacturing in Brisbane, seeking advice and quotations, until the manufacturing contract went to the Transfield company.

At the gigantic Transfield factory each of the letters was separately constructed in plate steel with an airtight base to minimise internal rust, and with thick bright red powdercoat as the paint.

It was only on site during the irreversible installing procedure that I realised my oversight in not noticing that the engineers had a 100mm base trench for the letters to sit into. The letters were now lower than I had designed for. Arriving at the site the following morning I found that an angled edge of concrete had been run onto each wall of each letter, creating a kind of 'lip' which was upsetting as a weakening of the concept. It was too late to change anything and I had to grin and bear my dissatisfaction.

Installing the letter 'D' on site at the Powerhouse Centre.

In the overall scale of the sculpture, which is 15 metres long, this is not immediately obvious and is an aesthetic nuisance rather than a blight, but these incidents are a reminder that as an artist working with commissioners, manufacturers and installers you cannot safely pass off a single iota of control to others. All elements involved with public art must be supervised at all stages, with the artist involved at every level, to ensure that the intimate specifications are met.

The following two photographs represent the scale of the work, its location and – importantly – its presence as and in action. The two children standing on the *F* and *L* turn to watch their friend climbing up onto the stem of the *D*, then sit talking on their letters. Is one photograph better than the other? I prefer the first (higher resolution) image because the children are held in a moment of suspense: we watch – as the two children do – a boy stretching to climb.

Watermark, 2000. Above image scanned from a 35mm slide. Right image is from a digital camera with 1.3Mb resolution (not bad, at the time).

This sculpture is meant to evoke the power of the Brisbane River sweeping around this curve at New Farm, triggering memories of the massive floods of 1893 and 1974, and anxieties about the next. The title '*Watermark*' means both a mark showing the height to which water has risen, and a design impressed into paper which is visible when held to the light, guaranteeing authenticity.

Text of metal plaque next to the *Watermark* sculpture.

A FLOOD IN BRISBANE, 2011

Flood waters in Brisbane peaked at 4.46 metres at 4am on Thursday, January 13, with 322 millimetres of rain received over the Brisbane River catchment for the five days.

On-line magazine *The Punch* reported on that day:

> "In the tonnes of coverage on the Brisbane floods, no one seems to have filmed or photographed the *"Flood"* sculpture by artist Richard Tipping on the river's edge at the Brisbane Powerhouse in New Farm. Perhaps it's already underwater? Do you know?
> **Update: 3:10pm** Thanks to social media now we know. *The Flood* sculpture now neatly marks the flood water line on the Brisbane River."

Yolande Norris's blog *Useless Lines* announced the same photograph as in *The Punch* as "showing an astoundingly prophetic public artwork by the text/art king." Gosh. There is now a small metal marker placed on the fence showing the high water mark.

Watermark has become something of a landmark in Brisbane over the years since its installation, with its minimalist conceptual leanings balanced by a solid sitting-there-ness: the comfy bulk, the glowing finish, and the relative permanence with a contractually guaranteed life of fifty years until 2050, one hundred years after my birth a month before 1950. This is a pure textual object in that it is not only an object carrying language but an object made only of language, with letters as solid forms.

Watermark under flood in 2011. These photographs are from an unsourced reference on the internet. There are meme-trails and origins are difficult to find so it's not been possible to give a photo credit.

WATERMARK IN THE SNOW

In 2003 a smaller version of *Watermark* was commissioned for the *Kunst:raum Sylt Quelle* (Art: Space Sylt Source) in Sylt in Germany on the coast near to the border with Denmark. The engineering drawings from Brisbane made construction simple, but I had no input to manufacture or installation. The length is about 8 metres. The Kunst:raum also has an *Airpoet* sign, from a large installation of my artsigns in Munich near the *Literaturhaus* (Literature House) in 1999. Visiting the Kunst:raum for an artist symposium organised by Galerie Seippel in 2003, this was the printed statement:

- Poetry is language dancing to its own music.
- Some lines of poetry spoken softly have resonance in memory beyond all instruction.
- Art is for the eyes and touch as poetry is for the ear and the tongue.
- In daily business, art doesn't often look at writing, and literature doesn't listen to art.
- I call my word art works "artpoems", because they bridge verbal and visual dimensions.
- An artpoem brings word and image together like atoms making a new molecule.

Watermark in Sylt, from 2003. Collection of the Kunst:raume. Steel, length 8 metres.

WHISPERING FENCE

Whispering Fence is a collection of fifty eight pithy phrases engraved into hardwood fence pickets. Plain pickets stand between each pair of phrases, emphasising the relationship of lines as couplets in a vernacular poem.

When I began in 2003 it was easy to buy eighty jarrah pickets at a big hardware store nearby. Needing more, I returned a few months later to find that there were no more jarrah pickets to be had (a good thing, as the forests in Western Australia had been hard hit), full stop. I was grateful to find a dozen left-overs hidden at the back of the pickets section; and these were essential nine years later when additional phrases were added.

Whispering Fence is about language as much as the politics of identity, and the simultaneously open and closed world of the suburban life which so many Australians enjoy. The texts push and pull between welcome and go away in a conversation about colonisation, land rights, subdivision, neighbours, migrants, refugees, border patrols, tribalism, and us and them.

There is affection in some of the phrases with *blue rinse* and *blue budgies*, *blue collar* and *blue tongues*, alongside strident calls and muttered threats.

Whispering Fence was made for a solo exhibition at the Sydney Opera House in 2003, and was on display in a crowded foyer gallery called The Studio for months, along with a selection of the artsigns. After years stored in the backyard in long wooden boxes which became the home for a family of bluetongues, in 2012 extra lines using the spare pickets were added and the completed version was shown in a solo exhibition at Australian Galleries, Sydney. It was donated to the Art Gallery of New South Wales in 2015 in memory of my mother Barbara Kelly (1921 to 2001).

Pages 135-138: Hardwood jarrah pickets, engraved text, 150 x 650 cm (variable spacing). Engraving with the assistance of Graham Roberts, Newcastle. Photographs by Greg Weight. Collection of the Art Gallery of New South Wales.

Whispering Fence

fence in fence out
enclose exclude

safe on the inside
safe from outside

welcome stranger
this is not yours

we are not you
this is all ours

go get your own
home sweet home

the alarm is on
just ring the bell

security light
silent night

subdivide and conquer
fence sit defence

double deadlock
mortagee sale

property settle men
only emotion endures

garage sale this sat
domestic hardcore

blue rinse
blue budgies

blue collar
blue tongues

hello go away
knock knock

flaming galahs
all we immigrated

boat & jet people
sweeping changes

surreal estates
dingo + rabbit proof

free convict stock
bushfires + termites

white picket poverty
no public liability

renovation central
backyard landrights

tribal custodians
gossip in tongues

window watching
homeless vacancy

lawnmower sunday
suburban dreamin

razor wire asylum
population define

refugee spell queue
god save hooroo

sausages sizzling
undies on the line

family secrets
blinds drawn

street talk
every no one

lovely to see you
now bugger off

OOROO

Ooroo or *Kangooroo* brings together my established interests in road sign language and Australian vernacular speech, presenting absence as a tangible presence. "Ooroo" is a traditional Australian way of saying "See you later" (the word can also be spelled and pronounced 'hooroo'). The kangaroo has vanished, leaping away with a jump start, leaving an iconic outline in the air.

The 'kangaroo crossing' sign is a common sight on back roads and a favourite with souvenir hunters. It can sometimes be seen in the countryside with careful bullet holes as would-be hunters target representation over reality. No wonder the 'roo wants to escape that semiotic trap.

Ooroo is a palindrome, with 'roo going in two directions; however, kangaroos can't walk backwards.

Kangaroo is a real word, not an invention or misunderstanding as some have claimed:

> "The word derives from the Guugu Yimithirr word gangurru, referring to grey kangaroos. The name was first recorded as "Kangooroo or Kanguru" on 4 August 1770, by Lieutenant (later Captain) James Cook on the banks of the Endeavour River at the site of modern Cooktown, when HM Bark Endeavour was beached for almost seven weeks to repair damage sustained on the Great Barrier Reef. Guugu Yimithirr is the language of the people of the area."

Wikipedia

The best graphic depiction of the leaping kangaroo is on the Australian copper penny (1938-1964). The shape used in the *Kangooroo* sculpture is precisely modeled on this design, following the outline from a scan of a penny from my boyhood coin collection.

Kangooroo was first exhibited at *Sculpture by the Sea* at Bondi, Sydney, in 2016; and then in front of Australian Galleries in Paddington, Sydney, before jumping over to the new Barangaroo park on Sydney Harbour in 2017 for *Sculpture by the Sea's* event *Sculpture at Barangaroo*.

Kangooroo at *Sculpture by the Sea*, Bondi, Sydney 2016.

Transporting *Kangooroo* through Sydney CBD on a truck with a six-metre tray in 2017.
Note that the two signs are double-sided, reading from both directions. Photograph by Jasper Knight.

Installing *Ooroo* at Barangaroo, 2018.

Ooroo at Sculpture at Barangaroo, 2017. Photograph by Jamie Williams.
Retro-reflective vinyl on aluminium on integrated square aluminium poles.
Two signs with concrete bases, 501 x 312 x 13 cm and 375 x 220 x 13 cm.

Ooroo at Sculpture at Barangaroo, 2018. Photograph by Phillip Wadds.

Jump Start, a wall version of *Ooroo*, was a finalist in the Sulman Prize in 2016. Retro-reflective vinyl on aluminium, 170 x 170 cm (sign), 75 x 114 cm (kangaroo).

Top Paddock, 2016.
Reflective tape on perspex.
Edition 6 + 1 AP,
49 x 72.5 x 15 cm.

The existing *Ooroo* is rated by *Partridge Engineers* to a wind speed of 108 kilometres per hour (kmph). At both *Sculpture by the Sea* and at Barangaroo, wind gusts went to 106 kmph which was a little close for comfort but all was well. The worst outcome in catastrophically high winds is that the square aluminium pole on the large yellow sign would bend. The structures are strong and fully integrated as the engineering drawings show.

Most recently *Ooroo* has been chewing grass at Australian Galleries Sculpture Park near Daylesford in Victoria, while waiting for a permanent home.

As the pitch has it: "Kangooroo needs an outdoor home where the public can enjoy its serious visual and verbal play, engaging with vernacular language and with a new take on one of Australia's favourite symbols."

Upon sale, it will be made anew with full wind-resistance to at least 240 kmph (the new standard for wind-load capacity in Victoria) using steel square poles instead of aluminium and with a geared rotational mechanism so that both signs are always turning towards the wind.

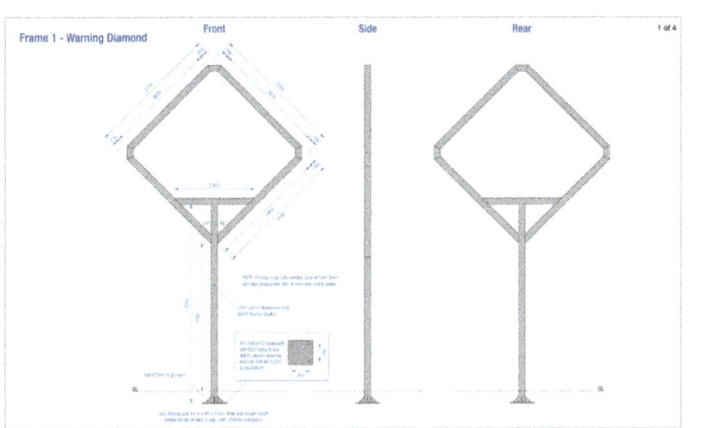
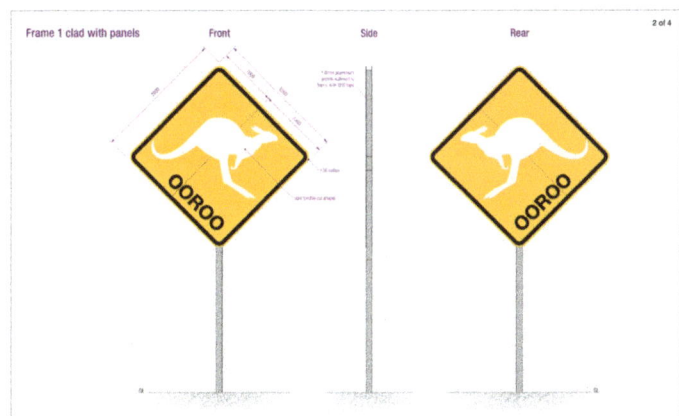
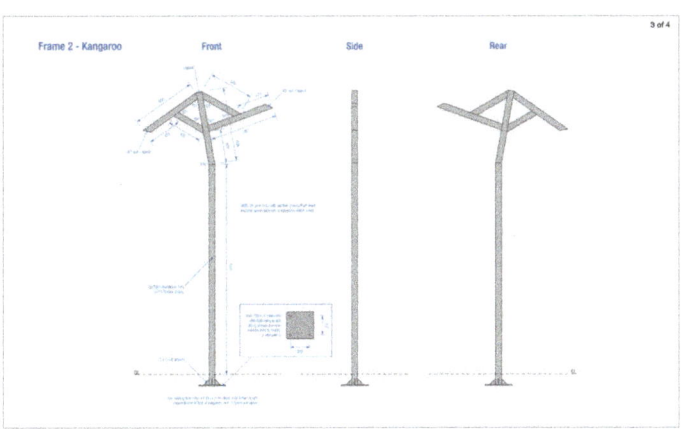
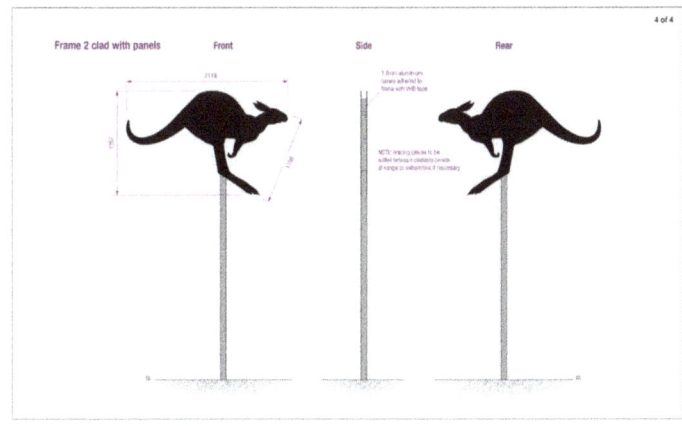

Ooroo at Australian Galleries Sculpture Park at Porcupine Ridge, Daylesford, Victoria, with thanks to Stuart Purves.

CANBERROR

Canberror Stencil, 1998. Plywood, enamel spray paint, 28 x 66 cm.

In 1997 I was invited to Canberra for a poetry reading by Hal Judge, and quizzed him about possibilities for a public art intervention.

> Oh Canberra ... I'm thinking of making a large-scale wordwork on sloping lawns in the city as an uninvited contribution to the Sculpture Forum in 1998, which will be
>
> CANBERROR
>
> What do you reckon? Know any suitable lawns? The idea is to have council worker's overalls on; carefully mark out the letters with string (at a scale to suit site and ideal viewing position = they might need to be 3 or 4 metres in letter height?); then spray lawnkiller onto the text, pull up the strings and depart.

Proposal to Hal Judge, May 1997.

Perhaps it was lucky that this didn't go further at full scale. In 1998 I hand-cut a stencil for spray painting, intended for footpaths. It was used instead to print cardboard signs.

This photograph of the stencil was printed independently as a large postcard for the Print Symposium at the National Gallery of Australia in 2015.

In 2018 I was invited by the director of *Contour566*, Neil Hobbs, to submit an idea for a large-scale outdoor work. After having made *Hearth* as a lawnwork in Frankston, I was hungry to go green.

Ref Canberror

Would there be a large slope of lawn available for a wordwork using giant letters of black plastic sheet which are pinned down with weed mat pins. After six weeks or so (and this may be for the opening as an EVENT) the plastic is removed and the grass is mown. Over months that follow, the grass recovers and slowly the letters disappear.

The slope would allow viewing/reading from a distance, and impact as a more public work than flat lawn. A Contour? The only problem might be convincing the guardians of the lawns to (1) allow their green surface to be marked (2) with a piece of hearty art humour.

Proposal to Neil Hobbs, February 2018

Neil Hobbs received permission for Canberror to appear on a big stretch of lawn which covers Canberra Contemporary Art Space next to Lake Burley Griffin, but with the condition that cut lettering not remain on the lawn. This conundrum was solved by using the cut letters as the edge-marker for white lawn paint usually seen on tennis courts.

The scaling up for each letter was from A4 to four metres square, using thick orange builders' plastic sheet.

I made the nine letters, each 4 x 4 metres, on lawn in my small backyard.

Mark Herbert was a great help with the installation, and the skies cleared for some hours. The nine giant sheets were positioned, pinned down, and photographed.

Scaling up the letters from A3 to four metres square.

Laying out the letters with Mark Herbert.

Canberror, 2018 with orange plastic, 4 x 40 metres.

Contour566 was a vibrant public art festival but the media in Canberra ignored *Canberror*. Who wants some outsider playing with your name? Thankfully the Federal government (LNP Coalition, 2013 to 2022) was thrown out a few years later. I like to think that *Canberror* helped to place some self-serving and visionless politicians into the pond of Lake Burley Griffin. They can use the letters of *Alphabet Soup* as lifebuoys.

Applying lawnpaint to the template outline for *Canberror*.

Canberror 2018 with lawnpaint, 4 x 40 metres.

WRITING ON ELECTRONS

When I made the *Everlasting Stones* shown in my first solo exhibition at the Adelaide Festival Centre in 1978, it was an adventure into the core of verbal particles, using few words. With *Writing on Electrons* I wanted instead to embody original poetic lines within a solid natural form, to open up a contemplation space for poetry which engages with mortality, place and the nature of both consciousness and language.

Writing on Electrons is a word sculpture made of nine basalt crystals weighing around three hundred kilograms each. These stones have an original four-line poem engraved on their one polished side.

My background in this field in the late 1970s had been filled with the sounds of grinding and sawing, within a gigantic factory and stoneyard. Four decades later, in 2007, I had control of design but could not be involved directly with manufacturing processes as such production had moved to China. It was a new century. I was fortunate to be able to acquire these basalt crystals, a rare form of this ancient material, from China thanks to the same John Hall who opened the pathway to monumental poems in the late 1970s; but now instead of a stoneyard he had a large computer screen. These crystals have an intense sculptural presence, so the words needed to be carefully placed and balanced.

I chose a font called – suitably – *Stone Sans* and then selected and adapted stanzas from poems in my manuscripts to make four line poems (they're like independent stanzas) with some emotional and rhythmic forward push. They are meant to work independently but also to gain from each other as a sequence which can be read in any order. The reader visiting the installation engages with the poems individually in the outdoors context where they are placed to be encountered.

Line-breaks help make the reader to **SAY** the poem, not just skim it. These poems have resonance in their voicing. The aim is to embody memorable language which can be remembered and passed on. Voice is the first state of poetry: as an oral art there is no need for an object. The stone becomes a kind of score, like notes of music written down as meant for performance. Poetry lives and breathes through its voicing. Metaphysical philosophy rocks, giving weight to words. The stones will each carry their poems for a long time to come

Writing on Electrons was unpacked from large wooden crates in 2014 and installed in the front garden of my niece Sarah Ward's home in the foothills of the Mount Lofty Ranges, where it remained for years. I tried to find a place for the sculpture with some key institutions in Adelaide but money for art is scarce and diversity is the new must. Then I worked hard in 2021-22 proposing a *Poets Way* in Sydney's Royal Botanic Gardens to link nearby Statues of Robbie Burns and Henry Lawson with Janet Laurance's anthology of eucalyptus poems on glass in a Poets Walk (originally proposed in 1926) with *Writing on Electrons* as the new addition to create a special place for poetry events. This proposal had the welcome written support of both the Art Gallery of NSW and State Library of New South Wales nearby but was firmly rejected by the Gardens for their own unstated reasons.

Morning, 2007. A second example of one basalt crystal was made.
This is now in the collection of MAC Museum of Art and Culture at Lake Macquarie.

Writing on Electrons (detail) in 2014 at its location for safe-keeping in the Adelaide Hills thanks to Sarah Ward and family.

writing on electrons, entering the bodies of the immortals
a shadow of the actual   midnight on the dot, in heaven
living by luck alone   the same things will still exist
we'd gladly be gods   but it would spoil the game

imagine silence and   solitude firm as bread
imagine hunger cutting   first slice, first breath
imagine silence, answering   each syllable back
imagine alone, around   yourself the only sound

animals made people: never forget that.   the earth
was helpless against sheer will   and a good idea.
cosmologies entwined: so eternity is in love with
the productions of time!   now you know everything

all creatures are aware.   intense existences

the crumbling rock escapes   ideas of time

and change   a single cell has planets and suns

all life emitting light   into interstellar dreaming

intuition thickens into presence: the senses
of animals, sniffing   and listening in the dark
life shrinks from infinity – beyond light no matter
your ego pops   under lack of pressure

is it into aeons   of nothingness we go
where time never starts   or float forever, bliss
in some brimming   immeasurable flow   and our
hearts   these wildest flowers   forget desire?

language binds us with invisible threads to the

translucent body of our illusions.   how can

a drop of water ever be saved from drying up?

the Buddha replied: by throwing it into the sea

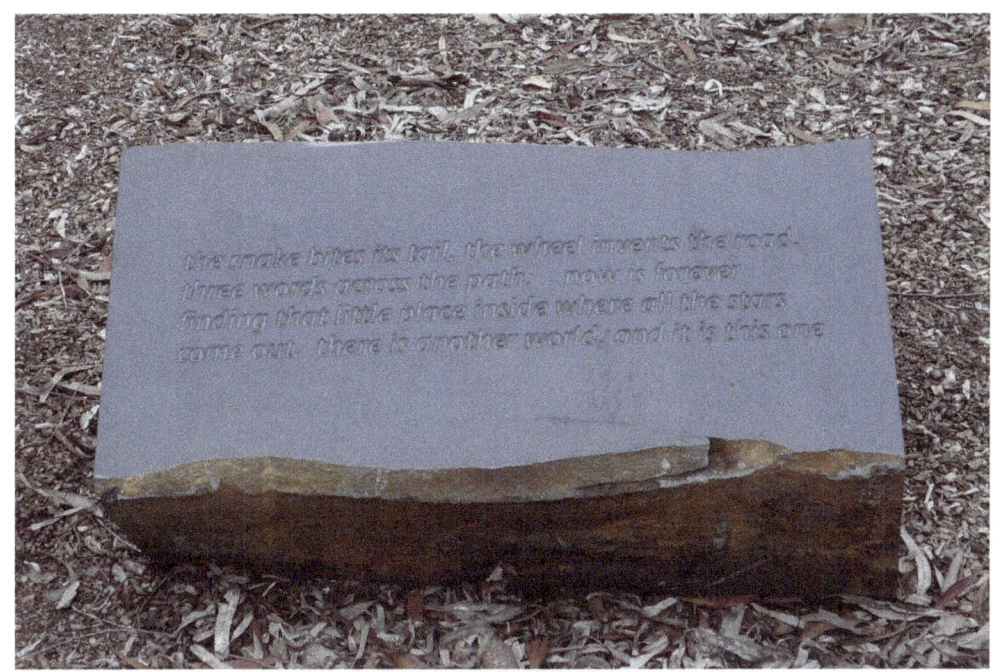

the snake bites its tail,   the wheel invents the road.
three words across the path: now is forever
finding that little place inside   where all the stars
come out.   there is another world, and it is this one

In 2022 *Writing on Electrons* was accepted by Heide Museum of Modern Art in Melbourne, with the stones to be set out in the garden of the old farm where radical artists roamed in the mid twentieth century. This is being made possible by the generous donation of Penelope Seidler covering the high costs of transportation and installation. Home at last.

A rubbing (frottage) made of one of the basal stones, (see picture of the stone at beginning of *Writing on Electrons*) using hand-made paper and a graphite stick. The public will be invited to make their own rubbings of the nine poems.

in the freshly unfolded   archives of

our sleep   all loves undone   in threads

weaving slowly   sun's dream   a golden

warmth   covers us with morning

Writing on Electrons

writing on electrons, entering the body of the immortals
a shadow of the actual   midnight on the dot, in heaven
living by luck alone   the same things will still exist.
we'd gladly be gods   but it would spoil the game.

imagine silence and   solitude firm as bread.
imagine hunger cutting   first slice, first breath.
imagine silence, answering   each syllable back.
imagine, alone, around,   yourself the only sound.

animals made people: never forget that.   the earth
was helpless against sheer will   and a good idea.
cosmologies entwined: so eternity is in love with
the productions of time!   now you know everything.

all creatures are aware.   intense existences
the crumbling rock escapes   ideas of time
and change   a single cell has planets and suns -
all life emitting light   into interstellar dreaming.

intuition thickens into presence: the senses
of animals, sniffing   and listening in the dark.
life shrinks from infinity - beyond light no matter.
your ego pops   under lack of pressure.

is it into aeons   of nothingness we go
where time never starts   or float forever, bliss
in some brimming   immeasurable flow   and our
hearts   these wildest flowers   forget desire?

language binds us with invisible threads to the
translucent body of our illusions.   how can
a drop of water ever be saved from drying up?
the Buddha replied: by throwing it into the sea.

the snake bites its tail,   the wheel invents the road.
three words across the path: now is forever
finding that little place inside   where all the stars
come out -   there is another world, and it is this one.

in the freshly unfolded   archives of
our sleep   all loves undone   in threads
weaving slowly   sun's dream   a golden
warmth   covers us with morning

COSMIC SEED

Cosmic Seed, 2000/2022. As a typographic concrete poem.

Cosmic Seed as an original visual concrete poem, a typographic wordartwork, seems so obvious that you'd swear you've seen it before. You haven't. I first made *Cosmic Code* in 2000, calling it either *For the Love of God* or *In the Beginning*, and made several versions either carved in wood or engraved into oval-shaped granite sheet.

In that year when I showed an early sculpture of the *Cosmic Seed* to an artist acquaintance who is a Buddhist he mocked it as a Sunday school illustration. Presumably he was thinking of how the Buddha viewed all of the prevalent gods as sentient beings trapped in the same cycle of Samsara and suffering as human being, deities being unnecessary in Buddhism. Suddenly doubting the veracity of the icon I put it aside for twenty years. Eventually I felt that my Buddhist friend was completely wrong. This typograph feels familiar, as if it has always existed, and yet is new and of its own kind (sui generis), waiting to be memed. *Cosmic Seed* doesn't belong to a religion, it is a completely free idea.

"In the beginning was the Word, and the Word was with God, and the Word was God." Let's take this to mean that it is the Word (language) which is our God.

Similar to the concept of a seed, 'cosmic egg' has use in astrophysics as a term to describe the theoretical moment of infinite density (a spacetime singularity) just before the Big Bang, as controversial as this instantaneous creation may remain.

In the Beginning, 2000. Medium density fible board on plywood, enamel paint, 16.5 x 14 x 2 cm.

The 'cosmic egg' has deep roots in many cultures' mythologies as an ancient concept symbolising the moment in which the creativity of God (name your god, 'godness' if you like) appears from the darkness of infinity before there was light and makes what will become life. Language is the essence of our success as social creatures capable of cooperation and compassion yet selfishly motivated as tribes often seeking to dominate each other.

The *Cosmic Seed* takes its own path through the uncharted gardens of Eternity carrying the Word as a creative spark without fixed meaning. There is a spirit in the world, as I've hoped to suggest in *Writing on Electrons*, which is beyond time and includes our common destiny.

In the Beginning 2000 + 2022. Scroll-cut medium-density fibre board on ply, acrylic paint, goldleaf, wooden frame, 55 x 55 x 5.5 cm.

Cosmic Egg, 2020. Acrylic paint on canvas, 122 x 91 cm.

Cosmic Seed, 2020. Wall work, with plywood back panel. Bluepearl granite, 51 x 38.5 x 3 cm.
One of a series of eight on various granites and of varying size.

Cosmic Metamorphosis, 2022. Reflective vinyl on aluminium.
Each colour set is unique at this size in a numbered series. 60 x 50 cm.

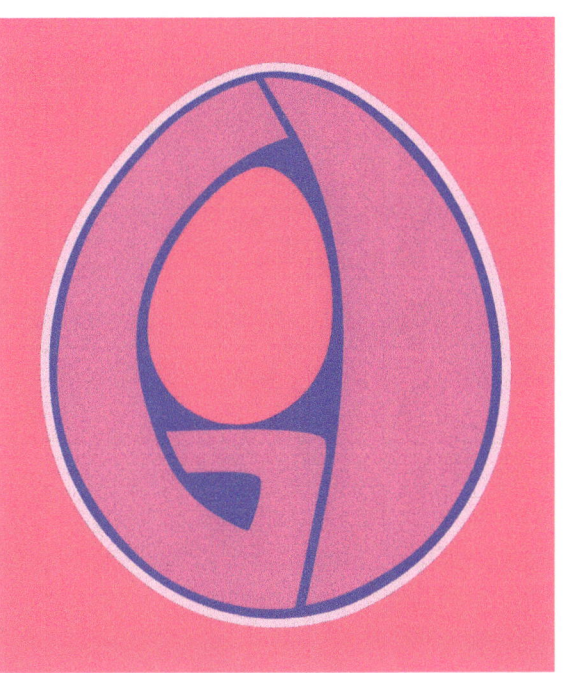

 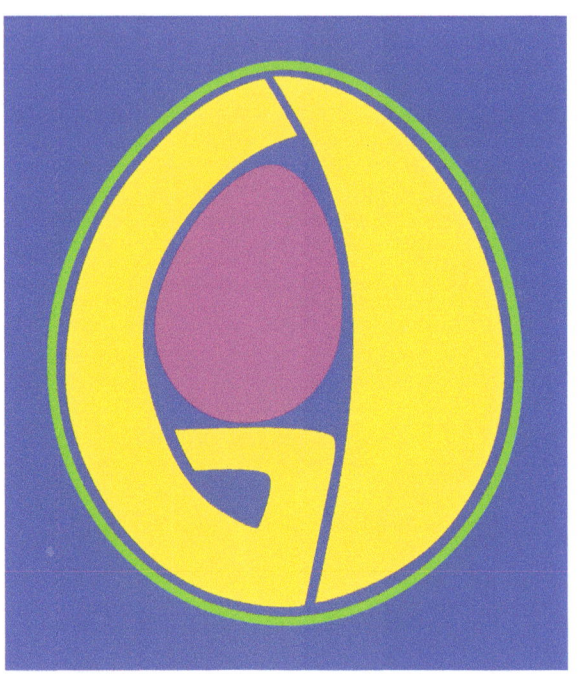

ACKNOWLEDGEMENTS

For my children Kai, Jasper and Grace, and grandchildren Mali, Lily, Rhapsody, Zephyryn and Manx. Dedicated to the memory of their mother and grandmother Mazie Karen Turner; to my mother Barbara Gertrude Kelly; and to my sister Susan Christine Tipping who were each there with encouragement so many times.

Chris Mansell has helped enormously over the past decade as my partner in literary art.

Writings here have been drawn from artist statements, journal notes and correspondence over the years but particularly from essays for my doctorate Word Art Works: visual poetry and textual objects (2007) at the University of Technology, Sydney. Norie Neumark gave valuable guidance, along with the early supervisors Stephen Muecke and Douglas Kahn.

Thanks to the editors of magazines which have included some of the sections in draft form including *Rabbit Poetry*, *Five Bells* and *Australian Poetry*. Visual concrete poems included here have appeared in *Meanjin* and *Contrapasso*; poems in *Southerly* and the anthology *This Gift, This Poem*; and more.

I appreciated the energy and skills which the book's designer Miranda Douglas brought to a difficult task, fitting a lot of fat rabbits into the tophat. David Musgrave of Puncher & Wattman has been a patient collaborator, letting this project grow at its right pace.

Many people are mentioned in the book, too many to list here, and I hope that this can suffice as their acknowledgement. I thank each one for being involved with these conceptual adventures.

Friends, dear friends, and all of those in our shared social world over fifty years of poetry and art, I salute you.

The Visual Poetics series features poems with a speakable visual-verbal structure on the page.

© 2022 Richard Kelly Tipping.

This book is copyright. Apart from any fair dealing for the purposes of study and research, criticism, review or as otherwise permitted under the Copyright Act, no part may be reproduced by any process without written permission. Inquiries should be made to the publisher.

First published in 2022.

Published by Puncher and Wattmann
PO Box 279, Waratah NSW 2298
puncherandwattmann.com
puncherandwattmann@bigpond.com

and

Thorny Devil Press
at WordXimage 445 High Street Maitland NSW 2320
wordximage.art

A catalogue record for this book is available from the National Library of Australia.

ISBN 9781922571076

Book design by Miranda Douglas with Richard Tipping and typesetting by mirandadouglas.com
The text is typeset in Adrian Frutiger's *Avenir Light*.

www.ingramcontent.com/pod-product-compliance
Lightning Source LLC
Chambersburg PA
CBHW041247240426
43669CB00026B/2995